1 - 28

# A
# Student's
# Guide
# to History

**Second Edition**

# A
# Student's
# Guide
# to History

*Second Edition*

## Jules R. Benjamin

St. Martin's Press • New York

*For Elaine, Aaron, and Adam*

Library of Congress Catalog Card Number 78–65211
Copyright © 1979 by St. Martin's Press, Inc.
All Rights Reserved.
Manufactured in the United States of America.
32109
fedcb
For information, write St. Martin's Press, Inc.,
175 Fifth Avenue, New York, N. Y. 10010

cover design: Edgar Blakeney

ISBN: 0–312–77002–2

# *Preface:*
# *To the Student*

The aim of this book is to introduce you to the study of history and to assist you in history courses. Whether you are studying World History, Western Civilization, Ancient History, Modern History, European History, United States History, or another historical subject, this volume presents some basic concepts and methods of the field and helps you acquire the skills you will need in your work. The revisions in the second edition reflect the suggestions of students and teachers who have used the first edition. It is hoped that these changes will make the book even more useful to you.

The first chapter discusses the purposes and uses of historical study and explains how historians investigate their subjects. A discussion of the various schools of historical interpretation has been added to this edition. Chapters two and three explain how to read a history assignment, take notes in class, give a classroom talk, and organize and write a book report or essay exam. An actual sample book report is included in the second edition. The fourth and fifth chapters treat a more complex matter—preparing and writing a research paper. These chapters help you choose a topic, use the library to gather information, organize your research, and present the results of your work in your paper. New to this edition is a model term paper which shows you how the techniques discussed are actually applied. Also new to this edition is a section on writing your own family history.

The appendixes contain reference sources and general information that you will find useful both in your present course and in any other history courses you may take later on. The appendixes have been greatly expanded and revised in the second edition to include more detailed information on many additional subjects, among them black history, women's history, Mexican-American history, Puerto Rican history, American Indian history, and immigrant history.

Throughout the book it should be clear that the study of history is not an idle journey into a dead past, but an aid to understanding and living in the present. The basic ideas and tools introduced here should help you make use of history to answer important questions about your own life and your relationship to the world. This use, in the end, is what makes history valuable.

J. R. B.

# Contents

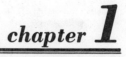

# The Subject of History and How to Use It

### What Historians Are Trying to Do

Since the time when human beings invented writing, they have left records of their understanding of the world and of the events in their lives and how they felt about them. By studying the records that previous generations have left, we can find out about the kind of lives they led and how they faced their problems. We can use what we learn about the experiences of people who lived before us to help solve problems we face today. Though the modern world is quite different from the societies in which our ancestors lived, the story of their accomplishments and failures is the only yardstick by which we can measure the quality of our own lives and the success of our social arrangements.

All of us look into the past from time to time. We read historical novels or books about historical events. We gaze at old photographs or listen to the stories our grandparents tell. Historians, however, make a serious and systematic study of the past and attempt to use the knowledge they gain to help explain human nature and contemporary affairs. Professional historians spend their lives pursuing the meaning of the past for the present. To amateurs, historical research is like a hobby, but their occasional journeys into the past may contribute to the store of human knowledge and can greatly influence their own lives. Your study and research as a student qualify you as an amateur historian. Your study of the past is part of the same search for knowledge carried on generation after generation.

### What History Can Tell You

Everything that exists in the present has come out of the past, and no matter how new and unique it seems to be, it carries some of the past with it. The latest hit recording by the newest group is the result of the evolution of that group's musical style and of the trends in music and society that have influenced them. Perhaps their style developed from earlier rock styles associated with the Beatles, or perhaps they are taking off from even older folk themes used by Bob Dylan. Well, Dylan was influenced by Woody Guthrie, who wrote his songs in the 1930s and whose music grew out of his contact with the heritage of American folk music from the nineteenth century, which in turn had come in great measure from earlier music in England and Scotland, some of which has its origins in the Middle Ages. So you can see that the house of the present is filled with windows into the past.

The car you ride in, although it may have been designed only a few years ago, carries within it the basic components of the "horseless carriage" of the turn of the century. Your car works because people who knew how to make carriages, bicycles, and engines put their ideas together in a new way. The knowledge necessary to make the carriages and bicycles came, in turn, from earlier inventions. Some, like the wheel, go back into the antiquity of human history.

Everything has a history. At least part of the answer to

any question about the contemporary world can come from studying the circumstances that led up to it. The problem is to find those past events, forces, arrangements, ideas, or facts that had the greatest influence on the present subject you have questions about. The more you understand about these past influences, the more you will know about the present subject to which they are related.

### History and the Everyday World

Most of us are curious. Children are always asking their parents the "why" of things. When we grow up we continue to ask questions because we retain our fascination with the mysteriousness and complexity of the world. Because everything has a history, most questions can be answered, at least in part, by historical investigation.

What are some of the things about which you are curious? Have you ever wondered why women's skirts in old movies are so long, or why Frenchmen often embrace one another whereas Englishmen almost never do? Perhaps you have wondered how the Kennedy or Rockefeller families came to be rich, or why the Japanese attacked Pearl Harbor. Have you thought about why most of the peoples of southern Europe are Catholic whereas most northern Europeans are not? Many oriental peoples bow when they greet one another; we shake hands. The questions could go on forever; all the answers are written somewhere in the record of the past.

The record of the past is not only contained in musty volumes on library shelves; it is all around us in museums, historical preservations, and the antique furnishings and utensils contained in almost every household. Our minds are living museums because the ideas we hold (for example, democracy, freedom, equality, competitiveness) have come down to us by way of a long historical journey. Though we are usually unaware of it, the past is always with us. Because history is literally at our fingertips, we can travel back into it without difficulty.

### A Brief Journey into the Past

If you have ever driven any distance, you have probably ridden over a system of very modern superhighways with high speed limits and no cross traffic or stoplights. This national highway network, built within the last twenty years, connects all the major United States cities and is known as the interstate system. These roads were planned by the Eisenhower Administration in 1955, and, though they are the newest highways in the country, they have a history that is more than two decades long.

Looking for the marks of history in the world around us is something like the task of the geologist or archeologist. However, instead of digging down into the earth to uncover the past, the historical researcher digs into the visible, everyday elements of society to find the historical roots from which they sprang. The fact that the interstate highway system built in the 1960s and 1970s had its origins in the 1950s is just, so to speak, the uppermost layer of history. If a study of the newest highways can take us back twenty years, what about the historical roots of the older highways or of the country roads? How far into the past can we travel on them?

Turn off the eight-lane interstate, past the gleaming Exxon station, past the orange roof of the Howard Johnson restaurant, past the bright signs before the multistoried Holiday Inn, and onto, say, U.S. Route 51 or 66. These are older highways, built mostly in the 1940s and 1950s. Being from an earlier period, like older strata of rock, perhaps they can tell us something of life in an earlier period of America.

When you leave the interstate system for this older road network you first notice that the speed limit is lower and that many of the buildings are older. As you ride along at the slower pace there are no signs saying "Downtown Freeway ½ mile" or "Indiana Turnpike—Exit 26N." They say "Lubbock 38 miles," or "Cedar Rapids 14 miles." As you approach Lubbock or Cedar Rapids, you will see motels less elaborate than the Holiday Inn. They may be small wooden cottages with fading paint and perhaps a sign that says "Star Motor Court" or "Stark's Tourist Cabins." Instead of Howard Johnson's or McDonald's, you may pass "Betty's Restaurant" or "Little River Diner." If you pay close attention to these buildings and do not become distracted by the more modern structures between them, you can take a trip into history even as you ride along. All of the older restaurants, stores, and gas stations you see were built before the large shopping centers and parking lots that separate them, and they are clues to the history of the highway on which you are riding. Places like the Star Motor Court and the Little River Diner probably were built when the road was new. Unless they have been modernized, they are relics of a previous historical period—when men named Roosevelt and Truman were president and when the cars that rode by looked like balloons with their big rounded hoods, trunks, and fenders. The diner isn't air-conditioned, and the sign over the tourist cabins proudly proclaims that they are "heated." This is the world of the 1930s and 1940s.

Now turn off the highway at State Route 104 where the sign says "Russell Springs 3 miles" or where it says "Hughesville 6 miles." Again the speed limit drops, and the bright colors fade further away. You are on a road that may have been built in the 1920s or 1930s or earlier (in older sections of America the country roads can go back a hundred years or more). Time has removed many of the buildings that once stood along this road, but if you look closely, the past is there ready to speak to you. The gas station here has only one set of pumps, and the station office sells bread, eggs, and kerosene. The faded advertisements on the wall display some products that you have never heard of—NeHi Orange and Red Man Chewing Tobacco. If you see a restaurant or motel, it may be boarded up because the people who used to stop in on their way to Russell Springs or Hughesville now go another way or may no longer live in the country but in a nearby city. However, many of the homes along Route 104 are still there. They were built when only farmland straddled the road, and they may go back to a time when horses and not internal combustion engines pulled the traffic past the front door. Such relics of early technology as old washing machines and refrigerators may stand on the tilting wooden porches, and a close look behind the tall weeds beside the dirt driveway may reveal the remains of a 1936

La Salle. As you stop before one of the old farmhouses, the past is all around you, and, although the place does not appear in its youthful form, a little imagination can reconstruct what life was like here on the day in 1933 when Roosevelt closed all the banks or the day in 1918 when the Great War in Europe ended.

The line linking past to present never breaks, and the house itself has a history, as do the people who once lived in it. In this sense, every house is haunted with its own past, and a keen eye can see the signs. Enter the house and you can see the stairway that was rebuilt in 1894, and in the main bedroom upstairs the fireplace, which was put in about 1878, the year the house was built. Perhaps the old Bible on the table near the bed notes the year the family came to the United States, and the dates in the early nineteenth century when the parents of the immigrants who built the house were born.

The story could go on forever, although the evidence would become slimmer and slimmer. You could find out from county records who owned the land before the house was built, going back perhaps to the time when the people who lived on the land were red, not white. In distance you may have traveled only ten or twenty miles from the interstate highway and it may have taken you less than an hour, but by looking for the signs of the past in the present, you have traveled a hundred years or more into history.

If you think and study about the passage of time between the old farmhouse on the country road and the gleaming service station by the interstate, you may come to understand some of the social, political, and economic forces that moved events away from the old wooden porch and sent them speeding down the interstate highway. The more you know about this process, the more you will learn about the times when the farmhouse was new and the more you will understand how the interstate highway came about, what you are doing riding on it, and into what kind of a future you may be heading.

Historians don't usually wander into history in such a casual fashion. They have to be trained in their methods of investigation and analysis. As an introduction to your own historical research and study, the next section will describe some of the tools employed by historians in their examination of the records of the past.

### How Historians Work

Like you, historians are challenged by the complexity of the world, and many want to use their studies of the past to help solve the problems of the present. The questions that can come to mind are numberless, and serious historical investigators must choose wisely among them. They do not want to spend a lot of effort pursuing the kind of question to which history has no answer (for example, "What is the purpose of the Universe?" "Am I a lovable person?" "Who is the smartest person in the world?"). Nor do they want to struggle to achieve the solution to a problem that is not of real importance. (Historical investigation can probably tell you who wore the first pair of pants with a zipper in it, but that might not be worth knowing.) The main difficulty facing historians is not eliminating unanswerable or unimportant questions but choosing among the important ones.

A historian's choice among important questions is determined by personal values, by the concerns of those who support the historian's work, by the nature of the time in which the historian lives, or by a combination of all of these. The ways in which these influences operate are very complex, and often historians themselves are unaware of them.

When the historian has chosen his or her subject, many questions still remain. For example, does historical evidence dealing with the subject exist, and if so, where can it be found? If someone wanted to study gypsy music from medieval Europe, and that music was never written down or mentioned in historical accounts of the period, then little or nothing can be found about this subject through historical research. Even if records exist on a particular subject, the historian may be unaware of them or unable to locate them. Perhaps the records are in an unfamiliar language or are in the possession of individuals or governments that deny access to them. Sometimes locating historical evidence can be a problem.

Having determined that records *do* exist and that they can be located and used, the historian faces another and more important problem: What is the credibility or reliability of the evidence? Is it genuine? How accurate are the records, and what biases were held by those who wrote them? If sources of information are in conflict, which is correct? Or is it possible that most of the sources are in error? Historians must pick and choose among the sources they uncover, and that is not always easy to do. The historian's own biases, as well, cloud the picture, making impartial judgment extremely difficult.

There are two basic forms of historical evidence: primary and secondary. Primary evidence records the actual words of someone who participated in or witnessed the events described. These can be newspaper accounts, diaries, notebooks, letters, minutes, interviews, and any works written (or otherwise recorded, as in photographs) by persons who claim firsthand knowledge of an event. Another primary source is official statements by established organizations or significant personages—royal decrees, church edicts, political party platforms, laws, and speeches.

Secondary evidence records the findings of someone who did not observe the event but who investigated primary evidence. Most history books fall into this category, although some are actually tertiary evidence because they rely not on primary evidence but are themselves drawn from secondary sources. When your own history research paper is finished, it will be secondary or, more likely, tertiary evidence to anyone who may use it in the future.

The problem of determining the reliability of evidence is a serious one. Secondary and even primary evidence can be fraudulent, inaccurate, or biased. Eyewitness accounts may be purposely distorted in order to avert blame or to bestow praise on a particular individual or group. Without intending to misinform, even on-the-scene judgments can be incorrect. Sometimes, the closer you are to an event, the more emotionally involved you are, and this distorts your understanding of it. We can all recall events in which we completely misunderstood the feelings, actions, and even words of another person. Historians have to weigh evidence carefully to see if those who participated in an event understood it well enough to have accurately described it, and whether later authors understood the meaning of the primary documents they used. Official statements present another problem—that of propaganda or concealment. A government, group, or institution may make statements that it wishes others to believe but that are not true. What a group says may not be what it does. This is especially true in politics.

To check the reliability of evidence, historians use the tests of consistency and corroboration: does the evidence contradict itself and does it agree with evidence from other sources? Historical research always involves checking one source against another.

The bias of a source also presents difficulties. People's attitudes toward the world influence the way they interpret events. For example, you and your parents may have different attitudes toward music, sex, religion, or politics. These differences can cause you to disagree with them about the value of a rock concert, a Sunday sermon, or the president. Historians have their own attitudes toward the subjects they are investigating, and these cause them to draw different conclusions about the character and importance of religious, political, intellectual, and other movements. Later historians must take these biases into account when weighing the reliability of evidence.

In analyzing the evidence, the historian must find some way of organizing it so that he or she can make clear its meaning. A mass of facts and opinions concerning a subject is not a historical study. The task of the trained historian is to arrange the material so that it supports a particular conclusion. This conclusion may have been in the historian's mind at the outset, or it might be the result of investigation. If the evidence does not appear to support the conclusion, however, then the historian must either change that conclusion or seek other evidence to support it.

Once a historian is satisfied that research has uncovered sufficient evidence to support a particular conclusion, then he or she works to display the evidence in a manner that

will clearly show that the conclusion drawn is a proper
one. If any evidence that leads to other conclusions is uncovered, the historian has a responsibility to include it. In
doing so, he or she must show how the supporting evidence is stronger than the nonsupporting evidence. There
are many ways of organizing evidence in support of a conclusion. The historian's arguments in favor of a particular
conclusion must be strong and convincing, and the logic of
these arguments must not be faulty.

Recently, in an effort to eliminate error, bias, and faulty
logic as much as possible, some historians have turned to
techniques from mathematics and science to handle historical evidence and test conclusions. These historians
prefer to deal with quantitative or uniform data that are
easily comparable and that can be interpreted by mathematical formulas. Such researchers often use computers to
analyze their data. They question historical findings involving opinion and judgment and look to types of evidence (usually statistical) that can test the more intuitive
conclusions of other historians. The kinds of problems
they deal with are usually narrow, and they have to be
well trained in techniques of statistical analysis. Their
tests of evidence are sophisticated and are becoming more
so. The extent to which the study of history can or should
become "scientific" is an important current debate among
historians. (For some sources on quantitative historical
data see Appendix A, section 8, page 142.)

### Schools of Historical Interpretation

Historians investigate the questions they choose to
study in many ways. Their particular approach depends on
their academic training and their belief about which aspects of human nature and the human environment are
most important to an understanding of their subject. Tradi-
tionally, historians have been divided into those who saw
social, cultural, intellectual, political, diplomatic, economic, or psychological matters as central to answering the
question being investigated. The social historian investigates the development of human groups and communities
and their interaction with the larger society in which they

emerge. The cultural and intellectual historian deals with the meaning of ideas and attitudes and their effect upon social changes. The political historian focuses on the operation and acts of governments, parties, and institutions, whereas diplomatic historians deal with relations between governments. The economic historian studies developments in technology, production, consumption, and the division of wealth. Most recently, a group known as psychohistorians have centered their investigations on the emotional development of individuals and families.

Historical investigations can lead to very different results depending upon the aspect of human nature or society emphasized. Even greater differences in conclusions can result from historical investigations that employ different *philosophies* of history.

A philosophy of history is an explanation not only of the most important causes of specific events but of the broadest developments in human affairs. It explains the *forces* of history, what moves them, and in what direction they are headed. The dominant philosophy of history of a particular age is that which most closely reflects the beliefs and values of that age. Most of the historians writing at that time will write from the perspective of that philosophy of history.

We will look now at some of the principal philosophies of history, those which have prevailed over long periods of Western civilization.

Perhaps the oldest philosophy of history is the *Cyclical School*. According to this view, events reoccur periodically. This school holds the belief, in short, that history repeats itself. The essential forces of nature and of human nature are changeless, causing past patterns of events to repeat themselves endlessly. As the saying goes, "There is nothing new under the sun." This view of history was dominant in ancient times and until the rise of Christianity.

A central message of early Christianity was the uniqueness of the life, death, and resurrection of Jesus Christ. In societies influenced by the Christian Church—and especially in Europe in the Middle Ages—the new concept of divine intervention to overthrow the past weakened the

cyclical view.[1] The resulting philosophy of history, the
*Providential School,* held that the course of history was
determined by God. The ebb and flow of historical events
represent struggle between forces of good and evil. These
struggles are protracted, but the eventual victory of good is
foreseen.

This particular idea of the Providential School—that history is characterized not by ceaseless repetition but by
direction and purpose—became an element in the thinking of the more secular age after the eighteenth century. In
this new age of scientific inquiry and material advancement there arose the *Progressive School,* whose central
belief was that human history illustrates not endless cycles
but continual progress. According to this school, the situation of mankind is constantly improving. Moreover, this
improvement results not from divine providence but from
the efforts of human beings themselves. Each generation
builds upon the learning and improvements of those preceding it and, in doing so, reaches a higher stage of civilization. This idea of history as continual progress is still
very powerful today.[2] Currently, many variations of the
progressive philosophy share the field of historical investigation. Should you be interested in this subject, your instructor will be able to introduce you to the field of historiography (the study of the methods and interpretations of
historians) and to the works of philosophers of history
themselves.

[1] An earlier development of this new view is found in the Old Testament.
[2] One of the most influential of the progress theories is the dialectical
materialism of Karl Marx.

# chapter 2

# How to Read a History Assignment and Take Notes in Class

### How to Read a History Assignment

Reading history can be a satisfying experience, but to enjoy the landscape you must first know where you are; that is, you must have a general sense of the subject and of the manner in which it is being presented. If you begin reading before you get your bearings, you may become lost in a forest of unfamiliar facts and interpretations. Before beginning any reading assignment, look over the entire book. Read the preface or introduction. This should tell you something about the author and his or her purpose in writing the work. Then read the table of contents to get a sense of the way in which the author has organized the subject. Next, skim the chapters themselves, reading subheadings and glancing at illustrations and graphed material. If you have the time, preread the book or sections of it (especially the introductory and concluding chapters) rapidly before reading the full work.

The most common history assignment is the reading of a textbook. Many students hope to get by with their lecture notes, and they put off reading the text until just before the final exam. Reading the text week by week will give you the background knowledge necessary to understand the lectures and supplementary readings. In most courses the lectures embellish portions of the text, and lecturers assume that students are familiar with it. Sitting through a lecture on the economic aspects of the American Revolution will be confusing if you have not read the textbook discussion of the mercantilist theories behind many of the colonists' grievances.

Read the text chapters in close conjunction with the lectures to which they are related. Note the most prominent factual information and underline it. Also underline important generalizations, interpretations, and conclusions. Don't skip maps, charts, or diagrams. You are urged not to mark up library books, but the reverse is recommended for books that you own. Almost every page of the book should have some underlining on it. But don't stop there. When you come across a passage that makes an important point, illustrates the author's values, or contains statements with which you disagree, write your reaction or a summary of the passage in the margin. All of this will come in handy when you prepare to take a test. You will be able to reread the underlined material and your comments and obtain a quick review of the chapter's contents. Before the final, however, you may need to reread the text itself, especially if you are having difficulty in the course or wish to write an outstanding exam.

Another typical reading assignment is a historical novel or a monograph (a specialized history work on a particular subject). In addition to the procedures used in reading a textbook, you will need to pay special attention to the theme and point of view of these works. They should be read more carefully because your teacher will expect you to learn not only about the subject they deal with but about the emphasis and methods of the work. Therefore, you will need to determine the author's assumptions and values, and to understand the book's thesis and conclusions. Read this kind of work not only to absorb the facts but also to analyze, question, and criticize. If you own the book, you can do your questioning and criticizing in the margins. If the book is not yours, make your remarks on paper, and also write down a brief outline of the contents. Then you can review your notes or underlinings before the exam instead of rereading the entire book.

Some courses also involve the assignment of a book of readings. These are usually a series of short essays (excerpts from larger works or from primary documents) that deal with a single subject. All of the suggestions concerning the reading of texts and history books apply here as well, but this type of assignment often calls for a particular kind of reading. Each excerpt usually discusses a different aspect or interpretation of the subject, and some are in serious disagreement. Teachers expect students to be able to assess the arguments of the various writers and on occasion to take a position in the controversy. Therefore, you must read this particular kind of book with an eye to analyzing the arguments of the different excerpts or to comparing their different approaches to the subject. A good way to do this is to briefly summarize the argument or approach of each selection.

To help you appreciate the differences among the three types of reading assignments, here are passages from each. The textbook passage is from Stephen E. Ambrose, *Rise to Globalism: American Foreign Policy Since 1938* (New York: Penguin, 1971), pp. 148 and 150. The monograph passage is from Joyce and Gabriel Kolko, *The Limits of Power: The World and United States Foreign Policy, 1945–1954* (New York: Harper & Row, 1972), p. 341. The readings passage is from an address delivered by President Harry Truman before a joint session of Congress on March 12, 1947. Each selection concerns President Truman's 1947 speech to Congress, in which he called for a $400 million military and economic program of aid to anti-Communist forces in Greece and Turkey. In the speech the president also advocated that the United States act to oppose Communist movements throughout the world. This idea became known as the Truman Doctrine. As you read these passages, take note of the different manner in which each deals with this subject.

*Textbook*

The day before, 6 March, Truman had begun to prepare the ground. In a speech at Baylor University in Texas he explained that freedom was more important than peace and that freedom of worship and speech were dependent on freedom of enterprise. . . .

The State Department, meanwhile, was preparing a message for Truman to deliver to the full Congress. He was unhappy with the early drafts, for "I wanted no hedging in this speech. This was America's answer to the surge of expansion of Communist tyranny. It had to be clear and free of hesitation or double talk." Truman told Acheson to have the speech toughened, simplified, and expanded to cover more than just Greece and Turkey. He then made further revisions in the draft. . . .

At 1 P.M. on 12 March 1947, Truman stepped to the rostrum in the hall of the House of Representatives to address the joint session of the Congress. The speech was also carried on nationwide radio. He asked for immediate aid for Greece and Turkey, then explained the reasoning. "I believe that it must be the policy of the United States to support free peoples who are resisting attempted subjugation by armed minorities or by outside pressures."

The statement was all-encompassing. In a single sentence, Truman had defined American policy for the next twenty years. Whenever and wherever an anti-Communist government was threatened, by indigenous insurgents, foreign invasion, or even diplomatic pressure (as with Turkey), the United States would supply political, economic, and most of all military aid. The Truman Doctrine came close to shutting the door against any revolution, since the terms "free peoples" and "anti-Communist" were assumed to be synonymous. All the Greek government, or any dictatorship, had to do to get American aid was to claim that its opponents were Communists. And the aid would be unilateral, as Truman never mentioned the United Nations, whose commission to investigate what was actually happening in Greece had not completed its study or made a report.

*Monograph*

What was really on the mind of the president and his advisers was stated less in the Truman Doctrine speech than in private memos and in Truman's March 6 address at Baylor University. Dealing with the world economic structure, the president attacked state-regulated trade, tariffs, and exchange controls—" ... the direction in which much of the world is headed at the present time." "If this trend is not reversed," he warned, " ... the United States will be under pressure, sooner or later, to use these same devices in the fight for markets and for raw materials. ... It is not the American way. It is not the way to peace."[16] ...

The question of how best to sell the new crusade perplexed the administration, not the least because Greece was a paltry excuse for a vast undertaking of which it "was only a beginning," and in the end it formulated diverse reasons as the need required.[18] The many drafts that were drawn up before the final Truman Doctrine speech was delivered to Congress on March 12 are interesting in that they reveal more accu-

[16]DSB, March 16, 1947, 484. See also Acheson, *Present at Creation*, 219; Jones, *Fifteen Weeks*, 139–42.
[18]Acheson, *Present at Creation*, 221.

rately than the speech itself the true concerns of
Washington. Members of the cabinet and other
top officials who considered the matter before
the twelfth understood very clearly that the
United States was now defining a strategy and
budget appropriate to its new global commit-
ments—interests that the collapse of British
power had made even more exclusively American—and that far greater involvement in other
countries was now pending at least on the economic level.

Quite apart from the belligerent tone of the
drafts were the references to " . . . a world-wide
trend away from the system of free enterprise
toward state-controlled economies," which the
State Department's speech writers thought
"gravely threatened" American interests. No less
significant was the mention of the "great natural
resources" of the Middle East at stake.

*Readings (excerpt from speech)*

The very existence of the Greek state is today
threatened by the terrorist activities of several
thousand armed men, led by Communists, who
defy the government's authority at a number of
points, particularly along the northern bounda-
ries. . . .

Meanwhile, the Greek Government is unable
to cope with the situation. The Greek army is
small and poorly equipped. It needs supplies
and equipment if it is to restore authority to the
government throughout Greek territory.

Greece must have assistance if it is to become a
self-supporting and self-respecting democracy.

The United States must supply this assistance. . . .

At the present moment in world history nearly
every nation must choose between alternative
ways of life. The choice is too often not a free one.

One way of life is based upon the will of the

majority, and is distinguished by free institutions, representative government, free elections, guarantees of individual liberty, freedom of speech and religion, and freedom from political oppression.

The second way of life is based upon the will of a minority forcibly imposed upon the majority. It relies upon terror and oppression, a controlled press and radio, fixed elections, and the suppression of personal freedoms.

I believe that it must be the policy of the United States to support free peoples who are resisting attempted subjugation by armed minorities or by outside pressures. . . .

It is necessary only to glance at a map to realize that the survival and integrity of the Greek nation are of grave importance in a much wider situation. If Greece should fall under the control of an armed minority, the effect upon its neighbor, Turkey, would be immediate and serious. Confusion and disorder might well spread throughout the entire Middle East.

Moreover, the disappearance of Greece as an independent state would have a profound effect upon those countries in Europe whose peoples are struggling against great difficulties to maintain their freedoms and their independence while they repair the damages of war. . . .

The free peoples of the world look to us for support in maintaining their freedoms.

If we falter in our leadership, we may endanger the peace of the world—and we shall surely endanger the welfare of this Nation.

Great responsibilities have been placed upon us by the swift movement of events.

I am confident that the Congress will face these responsibilities squarely.

Note that the textbook is general in its coverage. It does not use footnotes or quote from primary sources other than

Truman's speech. It tries to summarize the content and meaning of the event without too much detail and without extensive proof for its conclusions. The monograph, on the other hand, covers a smaller portion of the topic, but it gives more detail, quotes from primary materials, and uses footnotes to record its sources of information. The selection from the book of readings is a primary source—the Truman speech itself. Often these books are composed of the original documents that form the basis of the historical events discussed by textbooks and monographs. Although this particular selection from a book of readings is a primary document, such works, as already noted, may also be collections of short essays or excerpts from monographs.

### How to Take Notes in Class

The first rule concerning note taking is simple: pay attention. Don't sleep, doodle, talk, stare out the window, or write a letter to a friend. Some lecturers are not exactly spellbinding, but there is no point in going to class if you are not going to listen to the lecture.

Read the text before going to class or you may be taking notes on the material in the book. If everything the instructor says is new to you, you will spend so much time writing that you won't be able to get an understanding of the theme of the lecture. If you have obtained some basic information from outside readings, you will be able to concentrate on noting points in the lecture that are new or different.

An instructor is most likely to prepare exam questions from material that he or she considers most important. It is therefore essential in preparing notes to determine which points in the lecture are given most prominent attention. Some instructors are very open about their preferences and clearly emphasize certain points, often writing them on the blackboard. Never fail to note something that the instructor indicates is important. Other instructors are less explicit about their biases and values, and you will have to try to figure them out. Listen closely, and make note of those interpretations and generalizations that seem to be stressed, especially when they differ from the approach in the text. You should not feel obliged to parrot your instructor's interpretations in an exam, but ignorance of them will work against you.

Your notes should be written legibly and headed by the date and subject of the lecture. They should reflect a general outline of the material covered, with emphasis on major interpretations and important facts not covered by the text. It is often best to write on every other line and to leave a large margin on at least one side of the page. This will allow you to add material later and to underline your notes and write marginal comments without cluttering the page.

If possible, reread your notes later in the day on which they were written. If your handwriting is poor or your notes are disorganized, it is best to rewrite them. Check the spelling and definitions of any unfamiliar words, and be sure that the notes are coherent. Remember, your notes are an important source of information in your studies, and if they don't make sense you won't either.

To illustrate some of the essentials of good note taking, here are portions of two sets of class notes taken from the same lecture. The first example illustrates many of the common errors of note takers, and the second is an example of a well-written set of notes. The subject of the lecture was early European contact with Africa.

## *Example of Poor Note Taking*

> Colonization of Africa—People were afraid to sail out. Afraid of sea monsters. But they liked the stories about gold in Africa. The Portuguese King Henry sailed south to find the gold mines and he built a fort at Elmina.

> England and France want to trade with Africa. They begin trading. Competing with Portugal. These countries got into wars. They wanted to control Africa.

> China had spices. They traded with Cairo and Venice. The Asians wanted gold, but the Islams

stopped all trade. They fought wars about religion for hundreds of years. Fought over Jerusalem. The Pope called for a crusade. This was in the Middle Ages.

Spices came from Asia. In Europe they were valuable because the kings used them to become rich. They also ate them.

The Portuguese wanted to explore Africa and make a way to India. Their boats couldn't get around until Bartholomew Diaz discovered the Cape of Good Hope in 1487.

Most of all the Portuguese wanted slaves. They shipped them back from Africa. Columbus took them after he discovered America (1492). The Pope made a line in the Atlantic Ocean so the Catholics wouldn't fight. The colonies needed slaves. They sent 15 million from 1502 to the 19th century. Slaves did the hard work. They got free later after the Civil War.

Immigrants go to Africa from Europe but they don't like the hot weather and they catch diseases. The Dutch set up their own country at the Cape. Then the English conquer them.

*Example of Good Note Taking*

Early European Contact with Africa                History 200
                                                  10/22/79

  I. Why did Europeans come to Africa?
    A. Desire for gold
       1. Medieval legends about gold in Africa.
       2. Prince Henry (Portuguese navigator) sent men down coast of Africa to find source of gold. (Also to gain direct access to gold trade controlled by Muslims.)
       3. Portuguese built forts along the coast. Their ships carried gold and ivory back to Portugal (16th century).

   4. Then the other European states came (England,
      Holland, France, Spain) to set up their own
      trading posts.
   5. Competed with each other for African trade.
      (Will talk about rivalry next week.)
B. Wanted to trade with Asia and weaken the Muslims
   (The Muslims had created a large empire based
   on the religion of Islam.)
   1. Religious conflict between Christianity and Islam.
      Fought a religious war in the 11th–12th
      centuries—the Crusades.
   2. The Muslims had expanded their empire when
      Europe was weak. In 15th century they controlled
      North Africa and they dominated trade in the
      Mediterranean. They controlled the spices
      coming from Asia, which were in great demand
      in Europe. In Europe they were used to preserve
      meat. So valuable, sometimes used as money.
   3. Portugal and Spain were ruled by Catholic
      monarchs. Very religious. The Catholic monarchs
      wanted to force the Muslims out of Europe.
      (They still held part of Spain.) Wanted to convert
      them to Christianity.

I
M
P
O    } 4. The Muslims controlled North Africa and
R         Mediterranean trade. If the Portuguese and
T         Spanish could sail to the Indian Ocean directly
A         they could get goods from China and the Muslims
N         couldn't stop them. The way to Asia was the
T         sea route around Africa.

C. The Europeans wanted slaves
   1. When the Portuguese explored West Africa
      (15th century) they sent back the first slaves
      (around 1480).
   2. The Spanish conquered the New World (Mexico,
      Peru, etc.). (Columbus had made several trips
      for the Queen of Spain.)
   3. In America (the name for the New World)
      they needed slaves. Most slaves were sent to
      America.
   4. Indians died from diseases of white men.

I
M          ⎫    They were also killed in the wars. There was
P          ⎬    nobody to run the mines (gold and silver).
O          ⎬ 5. Sugar plantations of the Caribbean (and Brazil)
R          ⎬    needed labor. Cotton plantations in the south of
T          ⎬    U.S. also. It was hard work and nobody wanted to
A          ⎬    do it.
N          ⎭
T             6. 15 million (maybe as many as 40 million) slaves
                 were brought to work the plantations starting in
                 1502 until mid-19th century.
II. Colonization
    A. Immigration (why white people didn't come)
       1. They couldn't take the climate.
       2. There were a lot of tropical diseases.
       3. The Europeans didn't want to live in Africa,
          only run it.
       4. Only the Dutch settlers came. They set up the
          Boer states in South Africa. After them came
          British settlers.
       5. Frenchmen (some) settled in Algeria.
       6. Some English also moved to Rhodesia.
    B. Dividing Africa
       1. Whites began exploring into the interior.
          (Will discuss exploration next week.)

Copying notes during a lecture is difficult, and even a
good set of notes can be greatly improved by being rewritten. Following is a rewriting of these notes. Note how
much clearer everything becomes.

*Rewritten Good Notes*

Early European Contact with Africa              History 200
                                                  10/22/79

  I. What Drew Europeans to Africa?
     A. Gold
          There were medieval legends that there was a lot
        of gold in West Africa. Access to the gold was
        controlled by non-Christian powers (Muslims—
        believers in Islamic religion). Tales of gold lured
        the Portuguese (led by Prince Henry) to explore the

coast of West Africa in the late 15th century.
By the 16th century, the Portuguese had built
several trading posts and forts along the West African
coast and were bringing back gold, ivory, and pepper.

By the 17th century, English, Dutch, French, and
Spanish ships challenged the Portuguese trading
monopoly and set up their own trading posts.
This was the beginning of rivalry between European
countries over the wealth of Africa.

B.  Desire to weaken the power of the Islamic Empire
(Muslims), and expand trade with Asia

Conflict between Christianity and Islam was an
old religious conflict (the Crusades as an example
in 11th and 12th centuries). The Muslims controlled
North Africa and the Mediterranean. They also
controlled the spice trade from Asia. Spices were
important in Europe because they were the only
known way to preserve meat.

The Catholic states of Portugal and Spain wanted
to fight with the Muslims. They wanted
to drive them out of Spain and challenge the large
Muslim empire in Africa, the Middle East, and Asia.
They hoped to convert them to Christianity.
*The Muslims were strong in North Africa, but if
European powers could discover a way around
Africa into the Indian Ocean they could outflank
the Muslims and obtain direct access to the trade
with India and Asia.*

C.  Slaves

Portuguese trading posts in Africa had sent a small
number of slaves to Europe starting in the late
15th century. With the discovery and conquest of
America in the 16th century, a new and larger
slave trade began to European colonies in the
New World (America).

The native Indians of America died off (they were
killed in war and by European diseases). There
was a shortage of labor. In the 17th and 18th centuries the mines of Latin America needed workers.
Large sugar plantations were set up in the Caribbean

and Brazil and cotton plantations in the southern United States. *The need for laborers to do the hard agricultural work led to the importing of millions of slaves from Africa.* Somewhere between 15 and 40 million Africans were sent to America as slaves between 1502 and the mid-19th century. This slave trade made Africa valuable to the European powers.

II. The Colonization of Africa
    A. Immigration
        Because of the unsatisfactory climate and tropical diseases, there was no major European immigration to Africa. The only significant white colony was in South Africa by the Boers (Dutch) and later the English. There were smaller European settlements in Rhodesia (English) and Algeria (French).
    B. Dividing up the continent
      1. Exploration

If you reread the poor notes now, you can easily see how little of the lecture material is recorded in them and how confusing and even erroneous a picture you get from them. What is there about the poor notes that makes them inferior?

First, they are not organized. They do not even record the title of the lecture, the course number, or the date. If these notes get out of order, they will be useless. In fact, they are almost useless anyway. They are nothing more than a series of sentences about gold, trade, spices, Portugal, and slaves. The sentences are not in any particular order, and they do not say anything important. Even the factual information does not cover the major points of the lecture. Instead, it is peripheral information about sea monsters, China, Jerusalem, Bartholomew Diaz, and Columbus, most of which the good note taker wisely omitted. By paying too much attention to trivial points, moreover, the poor note taker missed or did not have time to record the principal theme of the lecture—the relationship between European-Asian trade and the religious struggle between Islam and Christianity. The poor note taker also missed another major point—the connection between the enslavement of Africans and the need for plantation labor in the New World. Without these two points, this student cannot write a good exam on this subject.

The good notes, on the other hand, follow the organization of the lecture and touch upon the major points made in class. The notes make sense and can serve as the basis for reviewing the content of the lecture when studying for exams.

These notes are not crowded, but well spaced so that material and emphasis can be added later if necessary. They also have a wide margin for extra comments and the marking of important passages. (Note the emphasis on B.4 and C.5.) The instructor had emphasized these points in class, and by making special note of them, the good student will be sure to master them.

The rewritten version, which eliminates certain unimportant or repetitious phrases and smoothes the language into connected sentences, is even better as a study guide. The greatest value of rewriting, however, is that by re-creating the lecture material in essay form, it becomes part of the note taker's own thinking. The mental effort that goes into revising lecture notes serves to impress the material and its meaning upon the mind. This makes it much easier to review the material at exam time.

### Class Participation

Many instructors encourage class participation, and some base a portion of the grade on it. Here are a few pointers for improving your ability to participate in class discussions.

1. Be familiar with the subject under discussion.
2. If a point is made that disagrees with your understanding, or if something in the lecture or discussion is confusing, formulate a clear question or statement in your mind.
3. If you don't get a chance to be recognized in class, bring up your question with the teacher when the session is over.
4. Teachers are not impressed with students who like

to hear themselves talk or who ask thoughtless
questions, but if you are interested in the subject
and have thought about what you want to say,
never hesitate to speak up.

### Giving a Formal Class Talk

If a course involves an oral presentation in class, you
must learn something about this type of assignment. Elo-
quence and effectiveness in public speaking cannot be
mastered in a week or two, but you can make a start by
taking such an assignment seriously and adequately preparing yourself for it. Reading from a prepared text is often
the safest procedure, but this can lead to a dull presentation. If you speak from notes, you will have to be
fully familiar with your subject and pay more attention to
getting your points across. Nevertheless, this kind of presentation will probably be livelier and more enjoyable for
the class. You should prepare your talk outline as you
would that of a short paper (see pages 33–34). Be sure that
you cover all the important points and that you present
them in a logical manner. A dry run before a relative,
friend, or roommate is recommended. Be sure that you
exhibit a knowledge of your subject because this is most
likely to determine your grade. Effective public speaking
is one of the most important tools of success in many fields
of work, and giving a talk in class is a good opportunity to
develop your skills in this area.

# chapter 3

## How to Write a Book Review or Short Paper, and How to Take an Exam

### Book Reviews

A book review is an essay whose purpose is to comment on a particular work or a series of works bearing upon a single subject. The most important point to remember about a book review is that it is a *commentary*, not merely a summary. Unless your instructor specifically requests that you survey the contents, a book review should spend little time outlining the material covered by the author. The bulk of your report should be an evaluation of the way the author handled the subject, and a commentary on the book's contribution to your understanding of the issues discussed. Your review should discuss the author's theme and point of view, as well as your reaction to them; evaluate the author's methodology (rules for organizing evidence); discuss the author's values and biases; and draw conclusions as to how well the author's point comes across.

It may be necessary to refer to specific portions of the book to illustrate your statements and conclusions, but it is generally not advisable to quote from it. If you know something of the author's life or other works, it is appropriate for you to make these a part of your critical evaluation. When you are reviewing several works on a common subject, it is also appropriate to devote a portion of your paper to a comparison of their use of evidence, their success in supporting their themes, and their respective conclusions.

The form of a book review is similar to that of any essay. You should begin by making a list of points you wish to make. If more than two or three works are involved, do not discuss each one separately. Choose aspects of the subject that are general enough to cover all of them, and then compare the books from those particular perspectives. There is no need to give an accounting of the contents of each book.

Once your list of central points has been compiled, you should take each one as the focus of a different section of your review. (Don't try to make more points than can be accomplished in a brief book review. It is better to make a few points well than many points poorly.) Each section of your review should explain the point, support it with your own arguments and with brief examples from the book(s) under review, and then draw conclusions as to the meaning and importance of the point.

Because a book review is generally brief, come to the point directly and confine yourself to a small number of supporting examples. It should be clear to the instructor not only that you have read the book(s) but also that you have thought about what you have read and have used your own experience and critical faculties in formulating your comments.

To help you to see these rules and suggestions in practice, here is an example of a book review of the work you are now reading.

John Q. Student
History 100
October 14, 1979

Book Review of:   Jules R. Benjamin
                  <u>A Student's Guide to History</u>

Benjamin's purpose, as stated in the preface, is to introduce students to the subject of history and to provide them with study and research skills.  The author includes sections on such matters as "What History Can Tell You," "How to Read a History Assignment," "Avoiding Plagiarism," and "Organizing a Bibliography."  These subjects and others are presented clearly and succinctly, often with examples.  It does seem, however, that Benjamin has only the beginning student in mind and thus explains some matters (such as how to answer an objective exam question) that seem to me to be common sense.

I found the most valuable sections of the book to be those entitled:  "A Brief Journey into the Past" and "How to Research Your Family History."  In "A Brief Journey..." Benjamin makes clear how history surrounds us if we only know how to look for it.  The section on family history was very valuable because I hope to conduct that kind of research next semester.  Nevertheless, I think that the author could have given greater attention to this topic, despite the need to cover many other subjects.

Benjamin's point of view is consistently student oriented, attempting to fill study and research needs

while still paying some attention to history as an
intellectual field.  Overall, the book is clearly of
the "how to" variety.  The discussion of the philosophy
of history is very brief, and only passing mention is
made of the field of historiography.

Perhaps the most successful part of the book is
the long appendix:    "Basic Reference Sources for History
Study and Research."  Here the author lists dozens of
different kinds of reference works (dictionaries,
encyclopedias, atlases, biography collections,
periodical guides,) and page after page of bibliographies
on specialized periods, areas, or topics in history.
There is even a section devoted to bibliographies on
"Asian Immigrant and Ethnic History," which saved me
a lot of time in finding books for my paper on "The
Chinese in Nineteenth-Century San Francisco."  The list
of sources in the appendix is very broad but seems to
be most complete in Benjamin's own area of interest,
which, I discovered by searching biography collections
of scholars, is in modern United States history.

All in all, Benjamin has created a useful and
interesting guide for history students.  I feel that
I now have a better understanding of the purpose of this
history course and, hopefully, can get more out of it by
using the skills discussed in A Student's Guide to
History.

### Short Papers

A short paper (about five to ten pages) is not truly a research project. It is more of a report or essay on a particular topic based on the reading of a half-dozen or so sources. A take-home essay exam is even shorter but is organized in essentially the same way. Many of the aspects of short papers and take-home essay exams, however, are themselves similar to the preparation of a longer research paper. (For the preparation of a research paper see Chapters 4 and 5.)

A short paper should combine a brief review of the works read in preparation for the paper with a longer development of a particular theme. The theme is the central focus of the paper, and all your references, arguments, and conclusions should be related to it. (For the development of a theme see pages 77–78.)

Before writing your paper, you should first go through the books you have read on the subject and list the most important factual or interpretive points that you wish to use in support of your theme. You can then arrange these points in some logical progression and write a paragraph or two explaining each point and showing its connection to and support of your general theme. These paragraphs (approximately three to six pages) are the core of your text. This core should be preceded by a one- or two-page introduction, the purpose of which is to explain your theme to the reader. The core should be followed by a one- or two-page conclusion, the purpose of which is to draw together and summarize the arguments that support your theme and explain the importance of the theme and its relationship to other important issues. (For more on organizing a paper see pages 78–80.)

When the rough draft is finished, revise any section that is poorly written, that fails to support your theme, or that wanders into other subjects. Check for spelling and grammar. Read it aloud, and, keeping your reader in mind, make sure your theme comes across clearly and forcefully.

The form of a short paper can vary greatly, and you should be guided by your instructor's suggestions. If footnotes are required, one or two per page usually are sufficient, unless you are advised otherwise. In a short paper, footnote only direct quotations and especially controversial statements. (For rules regarding footnotes see pages 94–99.) In general, a short paper should not contain lengthy quotations. (For rules regarding quotations see pages 100–101.) Regardless of its size, however, a short paper should contain a bibliography. (For rules concerning bibliographies see pages 102–103.) A short paper or take-home essay should be carefully and neatly written. If possible, it should be typed double-spaced, with adequate margins on all sides. (For typing form see page 104.)

A common assignment for a short paper is the "thematic essay." Although you may be given a choice (as with a longer research paper), the topic of a thematic essay is usually assigned. The topic is an important historical issue such as the effects of the French Revolution or the causes of the American Civil War. These issues commonly take the form of such questions as "Was American entry into World War I necessary?" and "Was the New Deal revolutionary or conservative?" The books or readings that form the basis of your research for this paper also are usually assigned. These works contain several selections—written from different points of view or using different historical evidence or methods—all of which deal with the central issue or question. When preparing a thematic essay, it is important to have the central historical issue clear in your mind and to be able to describe the major arguments and evidence of each selection in regard to that issue. (See page 15 on how to carry out an assignment involving the use of such books.)

### Essay Exams
Preparing for an essay exam involves mastering the relevant course material. You will need to employ all your skills in reading course assignments and in studying your class notes. To do well in such an exam you will have to demonstrate your grasp of the subject.

Taking an essay exam can be quite a problem. You don't study, you don't study enough, you don't study the correct material, you forget what you studied, you panic in class, you don't have enough time to finish, your stomach is up-set, you forget to answer a question. There is no easy way of dealing with all of this, but here are a few pointers to follow until you gain the experience necessary to over-come these problems.

1. When you are given the exam don't panic. Read the entire exam slowly. Gauge the amount of time you will need to answer each question. Then choose the question you know most about to answer first.
2. Don't write the first thing that comes to your mind. Read the question slowly, and be sure you understand it.
3. Determine how you will answer the question and the central points you wish to make.
4. Write these central points or even a full outline in the margin of the exam booklet, and, as you com-pose each sentence of your answer, make sure that it relates to one of these points.
5. Your answer must follow the question. Be as spe-cific or general, as concrete or reflective, as the question suggests. Never allow your answer to wander away from the focus of the question.
6. Don't repeat yourself. Each sentence should add new material or advance a line of argument.
7. Where necessary, refer to the facts that support the points you are making. You must also give evi-dence that you have thought about the question in broad terms. The mere relation of a series of facts will rarely earn you a high grade.
8. Toward the end of your answer, you may wish to include your own opinion. This is fine, even desir-able, but be sure that your answer as a whole sup-ports this opinion.
9. Always reread and correct an answer after it is finished. The pressure of an exam can often cause you to write sentences that are not clear.
10. Write legibly, or your grader will be in no mood to give you the benefit of any doubts.

11. Don't write cute or plaintive notes on the exam.
They seldom raise a grade and may prejudice the
grader against you.

A well-written essay answer is a combination of (1)
adequate knowledge of the subject, (2) clear thinking about
the points to be covered, (3) well-structured sentences, and
(4) complete understanding of the question. Following are
two answers to a sample essay question on modern Chinese
history. The first answer is very well written and deals
successfully with the four requirements listed. The second
answer is very poor and meets none of these requirements.

*Question:* Discuss the origins of the Chinese Civil War of
1945–1949. How did the differing political programs of the two contenders affect the outcome
of that conflict?

*Good Answer*

  The origins of the 1945–1949 Civil War can
be traced back to the rise of Chinese nationalism in the late nineteenth century. Out of the
confusion of the Warlord period that followed
the overthrow of the Manchu dynasty in 1911,
two powerful nationalist movements arose—
one reformist and the other revolutionary. The
reformist movement was the Kuomintang
(KMT), founded by Sun Yat-sen. It was based
on a mixture of republican, Christian, and mod-
erate socialist ideals and inspired by opposition
to foreign domination. The revolutionary movement was that of the Chinese Communist Party
(CCP), founded in 1921, whose goal was a communist society but whose immediate program
was to organize the working class to protect its
interests and to work for the removal of foreign
"imperialist" control.

  Although these two movements shared certain immediate goals (suppression of the Warlords and resistance to foreign influence), they
eventually fell out over such questions as land

reform, relations with the Soviet Union, the role of the working class, and the internal structure of the KMT. (The CCP operated within the framework of the more powerful KMT during the 1920s.)

By the 1930s, when Chiang Kai-shek succeeded Sun, the CCP was forced out of the KMT. By that time the CCP had turned to a program of peasant revolution inspired by Mao Tse-tung. A four-year military struggle (1930–1934) between the two movements for control of the peasantry of Kiangsi Province ended in the defeat but not destruction of the CCP.

The Japanese invasion of Manchuria (1931) and Central China (1936–1938) helped salvage the fortunes of the CCP. By carrying out an active guerrilla resistance against the Japanese, in contrast to the more passive role of the KMT (which was saving its army for a future battle with the Communists), the CCP gained the leading position in the nationalist cause.

In the post–World War II period, the CCP's land reform program won strong peasant support, whereas the landlord-backed KMT was faced with runaway corruption and inflation, which eroded its middle-class following. The military struggle between 1945 and 1949 led to the defeat of the demoralized KMT army and the coming to power of the CCP.

*Poor Answer*

The Kuomintang had a stronger army than the Communists, but the Communists won the civil war and took over the country. Their political program, communism, was liked by the peasants because they didn't own any land and paid high taxes.

China was based on the Confucian system, which was very rigid and led to the Manchu dynasty being overthrown. The Chinese didn't

like being dominated by foreigners, and Sun
Yat-sen founded the Kuomintang to unite
China. He believed in the Three Peoples Prin-
ciples. At first he cooperated with the Chinese
Communists, but later Chiang Kai-shek tried to
destroy communism because he was against it.
Communism was not in favor of the wealthy
people.

The Communists wanted a revolution of the
peasants and gave them land. They also killed
the landlords. Chiang Kai-shek worried more
about the Communists than about the Japanese
invasion. The Japanese looked to conquer China
and make it a part of their empire. Chiang
Kai-shek wanted to fight the Communists first.

After World War II the Chinese Communists
attacked Manchuria and took over a lot of weap-
ons. They fought the KMT army. The KMT
army lost the battles, and Chiang Kai-shek was
chased to Taiwan, where he made a new government. The Communists set up their own
country, and their capital was Peking. That way
the Communists won the Chinese Civil War.

Let's see the differences between the poor and the well-
written essays in regard to each of the four requirements
for a well-written answer.

1. *Adequate knowledge of the subject.* The poor answer
fails to indicate adequate knowledge in several ways. It is
too brief, omitting many important facts. It describes the
political programs of the two contending parties in the
most vague terms. It refers to the CCP only as the Chinese
Communists, leaving the impression that they were a
loose grouping of like-minded individuals rather than a
strong, well-disciplined political organization. It does not
even mention the name of the most famous leader of the
CCP—Mao Tse-tung. Chiang Kai-shek, the leader of the
KMT, is mentioned, but there is no mention of his political program or beliefs, other than that he was opposed to
communism. Another serious defect is the lack of chronol-

ogy. The answer jumps back and forth between earlier and later periods, and no dates are given for major events.

The well-written answer illustrates a good knowledge of the subject matter. The origins, philosophies, leaders, and relationship of the two contending parties are clearly described. This answer brings in related issues such as nationalism, Warlords, guerrilla warfare against Japan, corruption, and inflation, thus indicating a broader knowledge of the historical context in which the Chinese Civil War developed. The chronology is very clear, with events proceeding in proper time sequence and with all major events identified by date.

2. *Clear thinking about the points to be covered.* The poor answer is not organized. Note that the paragraphs do not make separate points and that each succeeding paragraph does not further develop the theme of the essay. Paragraph one is a conclusion rather than an introduction. The second paragraph goes back to the founding of the KMT, but instead of discussing the origins of the hostility between it and the CCP, it merely states that hostility came into existence. The third paragraph begins by introducing the CCP (though not by name). However, it does not expand on the CCP's programs and points of conflict with the KMT, but instead abruptly changes the focus of events and the time frame by introducing the Japanese invasion of China, which the last sentence of the paragraph only vaguely relates to the question. The last paragraph, instead of drawing conclusions about the causes of the Communist victory in the Civil War, merely states that it occurred.

The well-written answer, on the other hand, uses each paragraph to make a separate important point, and each succeeding paragraph further develops the theme of the essay. Paragraph one sets out the political programs of the two groups and the historical context in which the movements originated. The second paragraph explains the beginning of the conflict in the 1920s. Paragraph three discusses that conflict in relation to the Chinese peasantry during the early 1930s. The fourth paragraph discusses the

development of the conflict in relation to the Japanese
invasion of the late 1930s. The final paragraph summarizes
the effects of the conflicts and of postwar developments on
the outcome of the Civil War.

3. *Well-structured sentences.* Many sentences in the
poor answer are badly constructed either because they are
awkward or because what they say adds nothing to the
answer. Some of the awkward phrases are "the Communists won the Civil War and *took over* the country"; "communism was *liked by* the peasants"; "China was *based on*
the Confucian system"; "communism was not *in favor of
the* wealthy people"; "the Japanese *looked to* conquer
China"; "the Communists *set up their own country.*"
These phrases cause the sentences to be unclear, and they
keep the student from getting his or her point across. The
other major defect in sentence structure is repetitious or
irrelevant sentences and phrases. These are "Chiang Kai-
shek tried to destroy communism *because he was against
it*"; "they *fought the KMT army*"; "that way *the Communists won the Chinese Civil War.*" The sentences of the
well-written answer, on the other hand, are clear, and each
adds new material to the essay.

4. *Complete understanding of the question.* The poor
answer does not deal with the central issue of the question—the political programs of the KMT and the CCP. It
notes that the KMT was founded on the Three Peoples
Principles, but it does not explain what these were. Of the
CCP, it says that there was a belief in communism (which
is obvious) and peasant revolution (which is vague). These
are the only references to political programs in the entire
answer! It is obvious that the writer of this answer failed to
understand that the central focus of the question was on
political philosophy.

The well-written answer is directed to the central issue
of political programs and begins on that very point. The
remainder of the answer makes clear the relationship of
political programs to the origins and course of the Chinese Civil War as called for in the first sentence of the
question.

### Objective Exams

Objective exams call for short factual answers. The questions may be multiple-choice, true-false, or definitions and identifications. If a simple choice is called for, think carefully about the alternatives before choosing. Read the question very carefully and don't jump to conclusions. If definitions or identifications are called for, answer briefly and directly. If you know only part of an answer, put that down, but don't add unrelated material just to make your answer look more impressive. You will be wasting your time. Moreover, don't try to change the question into one that you *can* answer. You won't get credit for an answer to a question that was not asked.

Here are some sample exam questions.

*Short Answer Question:* What were the motives that caused European powers to explore Africa beginning in the late fifteenth century?

*Incorrect Answer*

They wanted to dominate Africa and get all the gold for themselves. Columbus wanted to take the slaves from Africa, but the pope said it would start a war. But the war didn't start and the Europeans dominated Africa.

*Correct Answer*

The wars between Christianity and Islam were an important factor. The Christian states wanted to weaken the hold of the Muslim religion in Africa and to convert the natives. They also hoped to break Muslim control of trade with Asia by finding a sea route around Africa.

Check these two answers against the example of good note taking on pages 22–26, and you will see why the second answer is satisfactory while the first is not.

Based on your reading of this book so far, answer the following objective-exam questions.

*Identification Question:* Progressive school of historical interpretation.

(Check your answer against the definition on page 12.)

*True-False Question:* The Japanese invasion of Manchuria in 1931 destroyed the Chinese Communist Party.

*Multiple-Choice Question:* The founder of the Kuomintang Party in China was:

a) Chiang Kai-shek
b) Mao Tse-tung
c) Ho Chi-minh
d) Kiangsi
e) Sun Yat-sen

(Check your answers against the good exam essay on pages 36–37.)

### Take-home Exams

A take-home exam is usually a series of short essays. The construction of your answers should generally follow the procedure for writing a short paper. (See pages 33–34.) There are, however, a few specific guides to this type of assignment.

Prepare your answer by outlining those portions of the textbook or collateral readings that deal with the exam question. Then list the most important points covered in these sources—generally two to six for each question. Compose your answer by discussing each of these points in some logical order. As with all essays, it is best to have a central theme.

A problem that sometimes arises with take-home exams is plagiarism. In such an exam it is usually permissible to paraphrase the sources used in preparing your answer. Be sure, however, that you write in your own words. If you use sentences from a book in your answer, you are cheating, whether you mean to or not. Copying from a text or history work is unlikely to get you anywhere. Your instructor knows that experienced historians write quite differently from students, and passages taken from such a source will jump out of the page as your paper is being read. Most instructors penalize students severely for plagiarizing. (See section on plagiarism, pages 68–70.)

# How to Research
# a History Topic

In basic history courses you may be called upon to do
historical research. If you take advanced courses, you cer-
tainly will be called upon to do research papers, in which
case the present chapter will be helpful later. Whether you
are preparing a short essay or book review or a long class
presentation or term paper, you will need to know how to
gather all the necessary materials and how to organize and
analyze your information. This chapter will survey sources
of historical information and will explain how to use these
sources most profitably. The chapter also includes sections
on how to record information and how to organize your
notes.

### Selecting a Topic

If you are given a choice of research topics, choose carefully. Doing research on a subject that does not interest

you can be very boring. Try to select a topic about which you are genuinely curious. No matter what subject, person, or event you are interested in, it has a history. Every subject can be studied backward in time because every event was caused by events that preceded it. A history research project can be made out of almost anything. Perhaps in the neighborhood where you grew up there was a very old building and you had always wondered about when it was built and what it was used for. Finding out what the neighborhood was like when that building was new can be an exciting search.

An ideal topic is not only one about which you are curious but one about which you already know something. Perhaps you read a book about Socrates and want to know more about why he was condemned to death; or perhaps you saw a movie about the Depression and want to know what it was like to live through it. Instructors are eager to help students who show a real interest in a topic. Your instructor can assist you in selecting a subject related to your interests that also suits the particular course you are taking.

### Formulating Your Topic

Once you have chosen a general topic (the Spanish conquest of the Aztec Empire, or the Reconstruction government of South Carolina) you should decide which specific aspect is most interesting to you, historically relevant, and most suitable to your limits of time and sources. You will not have time to properly develop a broad topic, and your sketchy treatment would not earn a satisfactory grade.

To pare down your topic to workable size, ask yourself what it is that you are most interested in finding out about. If your subject is the Indians of the Plains, maybe you are most curious about the practice of magic by the Blackfoot tribe or how the Cheyenne got the swift Arabian horses they rode. Be careful that the questions you ask are not too broad ("Why did the Roman Empire collapse?"), too narrow ("Who was the first person to sign the Declaration of Independence?"), or too unimportant ("Why are Ping Pong tables green?").

To help you in narrowing your topic, here are some suggestions. Suppose that your general topic is the Mexican Revolution of 1910. First, check a brief outline history of the subject in a good historical dictionary or encyclopedia (for example, the *Encyclopaedia Britannica* or the *Encyclopedia of Latin America*). The description of the Mexican Revolution in these works will likely mention its principal leaders—Francisco Madero, Pancho Villa, Emiliano Zapata, and Venustiano Carranza. Perhaps your interest will now be triggered by the recollection of stories concerning Villa's daring raid on a United States border town (Columbus, New Mexico) in 1916 and how the U.S. Army under General Pershing marched into Mexico to capture him—but never did. Or perhaps you have seen the Hollywood movie *Viva Zapata,* which tells the story (not necessarily accurately) of the peasant leader Emiliano Zapata and his fight to preserve the farms of the Indian villages in his native state of Morelos. If you have ever seen a photograph of Zapata (and they were popular in poster form among college students in the 1960s), you know his piercing eyes and look of determination. If your interest in the Mexican Revolution is now focusing on Villa or Zapata, you should next turn to a biographical dictionary. Here you will discover that Villa's real name was Doroteo Arango and that he was a cattle thief as well as a brilliant military commander. Zapata, you will learn, led a peasant guerrilla army whose aim was to recapture the land taken from their villages by owners of expanding sugar plantations. To flesh out a paper on Villa's military career or Zapata's land reform program (some elements of which Mexican peasants are still struggling for today) it is time to turn to the subject bibliographies in Appendix A of this book or to the reference section of your library. Subject bibliographies will lead you to individual historical works on the Mexican Revolution, and from the book and article titles (and the descriptions of their contents if they are annotated) you will be able to determine those which may contain information on the topic you are considering.

Though you now have a good hold on your topic and have a short list of works that seem promising, you must ask the questions: "Does my library have the works I am

looking for?" and "Does it have other works, not listed in
the subject bibliographies, on my topic?" Since your ability to research a topic is often limited to the resources of
your school library, knowing how to fully exploit its collection is a crucial skill.

### Finding Information[1]

The best way to uncover the sources in your library
which relate to your topic is to approach the task with
certain *key words* in mind. These are the words you will
use when checking the card catalog. Key words, in most
cases, will be the nouns that appear in the tentative formu-
lation of your topic. For example, if your topic is the partition of India, your key word is *India*. If it is the use of the
submarine in World War I, you have two key words—*submarine* and *World War I*. (Your first lesson in library language may come when you find out that some catalogs list
World War I under "Great War," or "First World War.") If
you have any doubts, consult the librarian to find out
whether your key words are the best ones to use. This is
especially advisable if your key words are very general (for
example, "*conservative* thought under *Louis Napoleon*" or
"*social legislation* in the early *British Empire*").

### The Library Card Catalog

The main card catalog is a central file of every book in
the library. Most libraries also include nonbook holdings
in their main catalog. There may also be a separate catalog
for periodicals and another for reference books. (If your
library is very large, it is best to obtain a guide from the
librarian.) Not all catalogs are organized in exactly the
same way, but most set up their book card files according
to author, subject, and title.

### Card Catalog Information on People

If your topic is mainly concerned with a particular person (the early career of Mohandas Gandhi), you will find
books by or about that person under his or her last name.
These cards are known as *author cards*.

[1]If your school conducts a library tour for new students, be sure to take
it.

Before you start out be sure that all of your key words, especially if they are of foreign origin, are spelled correctly. If you are looking under "Gandy" or "Ghandi" instead of "Gandhi," you will have trouble.

There are two kinds of author cards, one for persons (for example, Gandhi, Mohandas; Nkruma, Kwame; Davis, Jefferson) and one for groups that publish works under their own names (for example, United States Government; Republic of France; Bethlehem Steel Corporation).

When you turn to "Gandhi, Mohandas" in the catalog, the first cards will be those for books written *by* the author. These will be arranged alphabetically according to

### Library Cards: Individual Author and Group Author

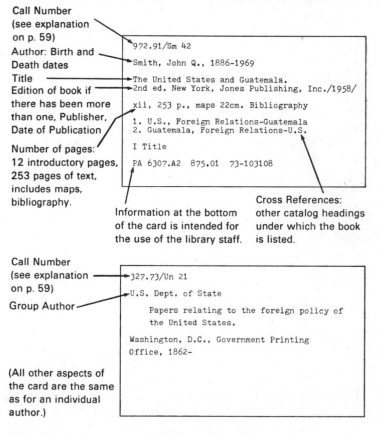

Call Number (see explanation on p. 59)

Author: Birth and Death dates

Title

Edition of book if there has been more than one, Publisher, Date of Publication

Number of pages: 12 introductory pages, 253 pages of text, includes maps, bibliography.

```
972.91/Sm 42
Smith, John Q., 1886-1969
The United States and Guatemala.
2nd ed. New York, Jones Publishing, Inc./1958/
xii, 253 p., maps 22cm. Bibliography
1. U.S., Foreign Relations-Guatemala
2. Guatemala, Foreign Relations-U.S.
I Title
PA 6307.A2   875.01   73-103108
```

Information at the bottom of the card is intended for the use of the library staff.

Cross References: other catalog headings under which the book is listed.

Call Number (see explanation on p. 59)

Group Author

```
327.73/Un 21
U.S. Dept. of State
      Papers relating to the foreign policy of
      the United States.
Washington, D.C., Government Printing
Office, 1862-
```

(All other aspects of the card are the same as for an individual author.)

title. If your subject is a famous person, right behind the books written by that person will be books written *about* him or her. These books will be listed alphabetically according to the author's last name.

Now you must determine which books by or about the person deal most directly and satisfactorily with your topic. The volumes written about Gandhi are very numerous and deal with much more than his early life. For example, a book entitled *The Assassination of Gandhi* is not likely to deal with his early years in much detail, if at all. One entitled *Gandhi's Role in the Ahmedabad Strike of 1917* will probably have too much detail on this one issue. However, because the strike was an important event in his early career, you may want to look at it. A book called *Gandhi's Influence on the Indian National Congress Party* will be a political study, and if your interest is in Gandhi's religious beliefs, it is not the best book to use. As you check through all the books on your topic, you will have to make judgments, based on the titles, as to which are most likely to contain the particular information you need. If a book title gives no clue to what aspects of your topic it concerns (for example, *My Life and Works*, or *The Career of Benjamin Disraeli*), then it is best to look at the book.

Another clue to the appropriateness of a particular book is the date of publication. For example, a book by Franklin Roosevelt published in 1936 cannot answer questions relating to his conduct of World War II. This system is not foolproof, however, because the date of publication can be misleading. A book of poems by Mao Tse-tung might have been published in 1967, but the poems it contains may have been written many years earlier. Likewise, a book on the textile industry may appear to have up-to-date information because it was published in 1978. Nevertheless this may be the date of the third or fourth edition of a work written in 1942, which, if it hasn't been revised, can tell you nothing about postwar developments.

Your ability to squeeze the last drop of information out of the title and date of publication on the catalog card will be enhanced if you know something about your topic to begin with. If you know, for example, that Gandhi spent part of his early life in the Union of South Africa, then you know that a book entitled *Gandhi's Fight for Racial Justice in South Africa* will deal with his early career. Again, if you want to write about the philosophy of Ralph Waldo Emerson, a book entitled *Emerson and Transcendentalism* will leave you cold unless you know that Transcendentalism is the name given to a particular philosophical school. The point is to be able to use the meager information on the catalog card to help you choose from among the numerous listings. If you remain in doubt about any particular book, look at the work itself.[2]

### Card Catalog Information on Places

If your key word is the name of a place, look under the geographical name in the catalog. This may sound simple, but be careful that you are using the most appropriate geographical term. Check a dictionary or atlas first to make sure that you are spelling the term correctly. The modernization of place names can be a problem (for example, Russia becomes the Union of Soviet Socialist Republics, Palestine becomes Israel, Persia becomes Iran, Peiping becomes Peking, St. Petersburg becomes Leningrad, Gold Coast becomes Ghana, Ciudad Trujillo becomes Santo Domingo). The card catalog usually will use the most recent name, but if your topic deals with a period when a particular place was known by another name, you need to know that name and to look under that heading as well. Another difficulty with place names is that some areas become absorbed into neighboring territory and take on the name of the larger unit. (Serbia is part of Yugoslavia, Ukraine part of the Union of Soviet Socialist Republics, Wales part of the United Kingdom, Zanzibar part of Tanzania.) When this happens, it is best to look under both names. Some areas have split apart, with the new units taking on new names. (Bangladesh separated from Pakistan, West Virginia from Virginia, Republic of Ireland from the United Kingdom, Singapore from Malaysia, Venezuela from Gran Colombia.)

Regional names also create a problem. If your topic concerns an important region like Provence (part of France),

[2]If you have been fortunate enough to find an annotated subject bibliography prior to your search of the card catalog, you already know the contents of some of the books listed there.

the Great Basin (part of the United States), the Atacama
desert (part of Chile), or Honshu (part of Japan), you will
have to check under both names. This is true as well for
important political subdivisions such as Umbria (part of
Italy), Alberta (part of Canada), Jalisco (part of Mexico),
Kiangsi (part of the People's Republic of China), Queens-
land (part of Australia). Knowing the correct and complete
name of an area is very important. Finally, be careful with
such geographical adjectives as "upper," "western,"
"southeast," "lesser." Some are parts of proper names;
others are not. "North Dakota" is a proper name and will
be found under "N," whereas "northern California" will
be under "C."

### Card Catalog Information on General Subjects

If your key words are general subjects, then your search
through the catalog will be a more difficult task. It is
tricky—like looking something up in the Yellow Pages,
where, for example, car parts are under "automotive acces-
sories" and toasters are under "electric appliances." If you
can't find a subject heading in the catalog to match your
key word, first check your spelling, then think of a larger
subject of which your key word is a part. For example, if
you can't find surgery under "S," it may be listed as a
subheading under "Medicine." You might find railroads
listed under "Transportation" and capital punishment
under "Law." If your catalog is well constructed you will
be aided by "see" or "see also" cards. If under "Wilder-
ness Campaign" you find a card that says "see Civil War,"
that means your subject is listed as part of that larger topic.
If you find cards listing works on your key word, you may
also find one that says "see also" and gives another subject. For example, if your key word is tariff, together with
the books on that subject may be a card that says "see also
Trade." This means that other books related to your topic
are listed under another heading. Unless you are sure that
the other heading is outside the scope of your topic, see
what is listed there. Many of the books may be the same,
but some will be ones that were not listed under the original heading.

*General Topics—Subheadings.* Extremely large topics ("United States," "Economics," "Plato," "Art," "Education") are broken down in the catalog by the use of subheadings. For example, the cards on "Argentina" will be broken down into subheadings like "Argentina—Travel and Description," "Argentina—Politics," "Argentina—Relations with Brazil." Some of the subheadings will be broken down even further; for example, "Argentina—History to 1800, History 1800–1900, History 1900–present." If your topic is the politics of Juan D. Perón, you should check "Argentina—History 1900–present" (because Perón was in power after 1940), and you should also check "Argentina—Politics." Because Perón is a well-known personality, you should also check for a main heading, "Perón, Juan D."

General topics are filed in the main catalog by *subject cards.* These cards are filed alphabetically according to subject heading. Within subject headings they are filed according to author's last name. The subject and subheadings will be at the top of the card. The remainder of the card will be the same as for the author cards.

**Subject Card**

```
Call Number →  N      Art - History - Modern
(see explana-  5300
tion on p. 59) J 14  Jones, Alice M., 1939-
               1970
                         A History of Surrealist Art,

                      3rd ed. Chicago, Acme Publishing/1970/

                      ix, 426 p., illus. 28cm.  Bibliography

                    → 1. Surrealism 2. Literature - Surrealist
Tracings ←
(see below)         → 3. Art - History - Modern  I Title
```

If you are lucky, the catalog card may contain a description of the contents of the book. If it does, as is the case with many older catalog systems, then be sure to note the book's contents because this is the best way to determine its relevance to your topic. If the catalog card is of the new type originated by the Library of Congress, it will not have any information regarding contents, but toward the bottom of the card it will have "tracings," that is, other catalog headings under which the particular book is listed. Though this information is more useful to librarians than to researchers, it is a clue to other headings and subheadings that might contain books on your topic. Whenever you find a book that bears on your topic, write down the tracings; if they seem like good leads, be sure to check them. Some tracings will be further removed from your topic. For example, if your topic is the atomic bombing of Hiroshima and you find a book under the catalog heading of "Atomic Energy—Military Use—World War II" that lists tracings to "Japan—World War II," this is part of your topic and should be looked into. However, if the tracing lists "Physics—Atomic Theory," this is removed from your topic and need not be pursued. The purpose of following tracings is to check every possible subject heading that might have more books on your topic. But don't get too broad in your search, or it will never end. (See section on budgeting research time, pages 72–73.)

### The Periodicals Catalog

Your library probably will have a separate catalog for periodicals or serials such as magazines, journals, and newspapers. This catalog has no subject or author headings and can be used only when you know the name of the periodical you want. The cards are filed alphabetically either by the name of the periodical or by the name of the organization that publishes it (for example, "American Academy of Political and Social Sciences—*Annals*," "American Political Science Association—*American Political Science Review*"). For a list of periodicals most useful in historical research see Appendix A, section 5, page 118.

Because this catalog tells you only which periodicals the library has and where they are located, you have to look elsewhere to find the articles that deal with your topic. Books that list periodical articles according to subject are known as periodical "guides" or "indexes." The reference section of your library should have several of them.

Different periodical indexes deal with different kinds of periodicals. Some, like the *Reader's Guide to Periodical Literature,* index popular magazines such as *Newsweek, Esquire,* and *Reader's Digest.* Others, such as the *Social Science Index* and the *Humanities Index,* deal with journals written for an academic audience. (For a list of periodical indexes especially useful in historical research see Appendix A, section 4, page 116.)

Periodical indexes have special forms of organization and use special abbreviations in listing articles. At the beginning of the index is an explanation of the subject organization and the abbreviations used. Be sure to read these pages before you begin to look for articles on your subject. These pages will tell you if the subject organization of the index is different from the one used by your library card catalog. If it is very different, you will have to master it in order to find out all the subject headings in the index that relate to your key words. Among other things, the index will explain the meanings of the abbreviations of the names of the periodicals (for example, C.H. for *Current History,* H.A.H.R. for *Hispanic American Historical Review*).

When you find an article in which you are interested, be sure to copy down in full the name of the author, the name of the periodical, the title of the article, the date, the volume number, and the page numbers. You will need all of this when you return to the catalog to see if your library has the periodical you want. Moreover, the library keeps all the volumes of a particular periodical together, organized by volume and date. Unless you know the exact volume number and date of the article you want, you won't be able to find it.

A special problem that you may encounter is that smaller libraries don't receive many of the periodicals listed in the indexes. If you come up with what you feel may be a very useful article but it is in a periodical that your library does not have, ask the librarian if it is available at a larger library nearby. There are many ways of tracking down materials, but always keep in mind the time you have to prepare your work. Don't spend too much time looking for a particular source; it might be better to look deeper into your own library's resources for other materials.

### Newspaper Articles

Some libraries catalog their newspaper collections in their book catalog; others put them in the periodicals catalog or in both. To find newspaper articles on your topic, however, you will have to go to *newspaper indexes*. These are published by particular newspapers and list the articles in the paper by subject and date. If your topic is the Geneva Conference of 1954, then you might want to know what a particular newspaper was reporting on that event at the time. One of the most complete newspaper indexes, and one that most libraries possess, is the *New York Times Index*. To find out what the *Times* was saying about the Geneva Conference, take the 1954 *New York Times Index* and look up "Geneva Conference" in the subject headings. Here you will find a listing of the days in 1954 on which the *Times* carried articles or editorials on the Conference. As with the periodical indexes, you will have to learn the abbreviations so that you can determine the exact place in your library's collection of the *Times* where the articles you want can be found. Again, be sure to copy down *all* relevant information.

Using newspaper articles as source materials can be very important. They are often on-the-scene and even eyewitness accounts of the particular historical event in which you may be interested. They can also contain detailed information on a particular occurrence that broad historical sources will not have. However, newspapers have their drawbacks too. First, because they are written just as an event is taking place, newspaper articles may contain inaccurate information. Second, they can tell you only *what* happened. To understand the historical significance of the event, you will have to read historical works. For on-the-scene accounts of what took place, however, there is often no substitute for newspapers. If your library's newspaper collection goes back to the years with which your subject is concerned, especially if there is an index to this collection, then it is wise to find out what those who reported the event at the time had to say about it. If your topic is broad, however, newspaper articles may not be as helpful to you. (For a list of newspaper indexes see Appendix A, section 3, page 114.)

### Nonprinted Sources

Many libraries have collections of nonprinted materials which can be useful for historical research. As technology progresses, new ways of recording the past are developed. Some of these are microfilms and other microphotography, still and motion pictures, sound recordings and tapes, and other oral history techniques. Check with the librarian to see whether your school library or one nearby has photograph, microfilm, tape, or oral history collections.

Photographs can be important pieces of historical evidence and motion pictures even more so. Oral history collections, usually consisting of recorded interviews or reminiscences by people who have been active in public life, can add both facts and excitement to historical research. Most libraries have a microfilm department where they store miniaturized photocopies of books, magazines, newspapers, and documents that the library does not have in printed form. These nonprinted sources are often filed in the main catalog along with printed works. However, it is wise to check for these sources in the special catalog that most libraries maintain. (For guides to nonprinted sources see Appendix A, section 9, page 143.)

### Reference Books

A reference book is specifically designed to give you particular information or to list works on a particular subject. Reference books form such an important part of your library that they are usually shelved in a separate place, often with their own catalog.

The reference library has books to help you find materials in dissertations, archives, atlases, other libraries, government documents, encyclopedias, microfilms, yearbooks, and other places. Many of these sources are specialized and will be of use only if you go on later to do more complex historical research. There are several kinds of reference books, however, that can be helpful in the kind of research you will be doing for introductory history courses. Most important of these are bibliographies, biographies, dictionaries, and encyclopedias.

Bibliographies are usually books that list a series of works on a particular subject. These are called subject bibliographies, and there are many of these dealing with historical works. (A list of the most useful subject bibliographies can be found in Appendix A, section 7, page 121.) These works can be used to supplement the books listed in the card catalog. For example, if your topic is Chinese nationalism in the 1940s, you may want to look at the subject bibliography entitled *An Interdisciplinary Bibliography on Nationalism 1935–1953*. In the section dealing with China you will find a long list of books related to your topic. For any books that interest you, copy down *all* the information. You can then check under the author's name in the author cards to see if your library has the book. A problem with this method is that, unlike your library's card catalog, subject bibliographies list books that may not be in your library. Some of these bibliographies are very extensive and only a large university library is likely to have most of the books listed in them. If you find a book listed that you believe to be of special importance but that is not in your library, the librarian may be able to help you obtain it from another library. However, this may take time, and you should be careful not to spend too long searching for one book.

Another type of reference work that may be useful is the biography collection. These books contain outlines of the lives of well-known people. They do not contain enough information on which to base a research paper on a particular person, nor were they meant for that purpose. But they can be useful. For example, if your topic is the New York newspapers and the Spanish-American War, you may need some information concerning William McKinley, who was president during the war. By looking him up in, say, the *Dictionary of American Biography*, you will find such information as when and where he was born, his educational and religious background, the various political offices he held, and even a short description of his role in the Spanish-American War. If a particular person is a minor part of your topic, biography collections can give you much of the information you need. However, if a person is a focus of your research, you will need to read works specifically devoted to that person's life. (For biography collections most useful to historians see Appendix A, section 2, page 110.)

You should use dictionaries and encyclopedias only to become familiar with the general outline of a topic. They cannot form the basis of a research paper because they only skim the surface of a subject. If your topic is the building of the Trans-Canadian railroad, you may want to get a quick introduction to the topic by looking it up in an encyclopedia. You may also want to get some general information on the geography of the region through which the railroad was built. For this you could look under "Canada" or "British Columbia" (or some other Canadian province) in an atlas or a specialized geographical dictionary. This general overview will help you determine which headings of the card catalog will be most promising. General knowledge of your topic will also aid in selecting titles that are closest to your subject. (See list of dictionaries and encyclopedias in Appendix A, section 1, page 107.)

### Locating Materials and Using Call Numbers

When you come across a book or periodical in the catalog that you think might contain relevant source material, be sure to copy down all the relevant information. (It may not seem important at the time, but if you eventually use the volume in your research, you will have to include this information in your footnotes and bibliography. If you don't get the complete data now you will only have to return to the catalog later to look it up again.) Also copy down the call numbers—the classification numbers in the upper left-hand corner of the catalog card. Without them neither you nor the librarian will be able to find the materials you want.

The call number indicates where the book is located. If

your library is one where only the librarian takes the books from the shelves, then you only have to write down the call numbers of the books you want. If your library has "open stacks," that is, book shelves to which readers have access, then you will need to know something about the classification system.

There are two classification systems in general use—the Dewey Decimal system and the Library of Congress system. The Dewey call numbers begin with a *numeral;* the Library of Congress call numbers begin with a *letter.* They are both complex systems, though once you master the principles, you will have an excellent road map to your library's shelves. If the stacks are open, obtain from the librarian a pamphlet explaining the classification system. Without the pamphlet you will waste a lot of time looking for the books you want. (An explanation of these two systems can be found in Appendix B.)

If you get to the place in the shelves where you think the book should be and it is not there, you are facing one of several problems: (1) the book is in use by another reader; (2) it has been transferred to another part of the library; (3) it has been shelved incorrectly; or (4) you have an incorrect call number.

When you find the book you want, it is wise to look at the books on the surrounding shelves because they will be on related subjects. Once you find a book, however, your search is not finished. Now you need to determine its relevance to your subject.

### Determining Whether a Book Will Be of Use
Once you have a book, you must determine whether it deals with your specific topic and whether its approach is appropriate for you. Book titles can be misleading. *The Election of Woodrow Wilson* may turn out to be about the inner workings of the Democratic Party. If you are preparing a paper on Wilson, this book may not be of much use to you, despite its title. Even when a book deals specifically with your topic, its handling of the subject may make it less than satisfactory. For example, a book that is written for less advanced students, even though it is on your topic,

will not make a good source. Its coverage will be general, and it may gloss over or omit important facts or interpretations that your research should include. A glance at the introduction should help you determine the kind of readers for whom the book was written.

Another problem you may encounter is the author's viewpoint or bias. For example, a history of World War I by a French author is likely to have a different viewpoint from one written by a German author, especially if the books were written close to the time of the war. It is very important for you to understand the point of view from which a book was written. Many historical events and their interpretation are the centers of profound controversy. It is almost impossible for a historian to investigate one of these controversial areas without the involvement of certain biases. A particular attitude toward the topic is not necessarily bad, however. Historical problems are immensely complex, and without a sense of which things are important, the historian will not be able to choose from among all the facts of the situation those that can give some clear meaning to the larger questions involved. In any event, it is important for you to become familiar with the biases of the authors you read so that you will not unknowingly accept their viewpoints. If you agree with an author's bias, it is natural that you will favor his or her work in your research. But unless you understand the biases of the authors you read, and your own as well, you will not know why you agree with some authors more than others. Furthermore, you won't be able to make a logical presentation in your research paper of the varying points of view.

The first place to check for determining the usefulness and bias of a book is its table of contents. Although some chapter titles are vague, most will give you a clearer picture of the contents than the work's title. If your topic is the Caribbean policy of Theodore Roosevelt, and you have come upon a book entitled *The Era of Theodore Roosevelt,* you will be pleased to find a chapter called "Hemisphere Diplomacy." Though the entire work may be of value to you, it is this chapter that will contain the most material on your specific topic. On the other hand, if the chapter headings are all concerned with Roosevelt's domestic policies or the cultural, scientific, and intellectual trends of the early 1900s, there may be little in the book on foreign policy.

If the chapter headings are not clear enough for you to determine the book's usefulness, your next move is to look at the index. Not every book has an index, but when one does, it is an invaluable tool. The index lists in alphabetical order the pages on which different persons or subjects are discussed. The index in a book on the Progressive Party in Wisconsin will list each of the pages on which Robert M. LaFollette is mentioned. It may even break this down and tell you which pages discuss LaFollette's early career, which discuss his campaigns for the presidency, and so on. When the scope of a book is very broad, the index is the best guide to finding that portion of it that is closest to your topic. Remember, however, that unless you read more of the book than just those pages which deal with your topic, you will not know the author's biases or conclusions, and these may be of great importance. Although you may want to select only small portions of a book to use in your research, if any of your own conclusions are drawn from a particular work, you will need to know its overall contents.

If the book has no index, or if you wish to get the flavor of the work as a whole before selecting it as a source for your paper, the introduction and bibliography may be of help. Authors often explain some of their purposes and conclusions in the introduction, and a look at the bibliography (if one is included) will give clues as to what sources the author felt were important and how extensive his or her own research was.

Perhaps the best way to gain an overall impression of a work is to skim its contents by reading the introductory paragraph of each chapter and perhaps the introductory sentence to each paragraph in those parts of the book that seem most important. If you have mastered a method of rapid reading, that skill will be very useful here. Once you have chosen a book for your research, of course, there is no substitute for careful reading.

### Reading Books

Reading books may sound easy but unless you have had experience in reading serious historical studies you may have problems. First of all, some of the vocabulary may be new to you. A book on the French Revolution will contain such words as Jacobin, Thermidore, and Girondin. A study of the atom bomb will talk about implosion and fission and such places as Tinian and Eniwetok. It is best to have a good dictionary handy. Another problem will be the academic or scholarly style of writing often found in specialized works. You will come across sentences like this:

> Despite the innumerable, and often contradictory, intellectual themes reflected in the ideological position taken by the right wing of the movement, it nevertheless managed, despite the defection of a small fascist element, to maintain the loyalty of the land-owning peasantry of the Central Highlands as well as the professional and shopowners associations of the capital, not to mention that of several union organizations which still maintained a craft orientation.

By the time you finish such a sentence, you may have forgotten how it began. To make matters worse, such tongue twisters are often filled with words like: balkanization, corporativism, Hegelianism, Mandate of Heaven, negritude, neomercantilism, Pan-Slavism, Pax Romana, popular front, primogeniture, Reconquista, shogunate, Trotskyism, utilitarianism, White Terror, or Zoroastrianism. Unfortunately there is no shortcut to understanding such terminology. As you become familiar with your topic, you will learn the meanings of the terms used by scholars. The only way to get through the complex prose is to have a good background in English grammar and a familiarity with the subject being discussed. Therefore, among the books you have chosen for your research, you should read first the most general and then the more specialized ones.

As you become familiar with the style and terminology used in a work, your main task will be to understand the points the author is trying to establish. All good works of

history do more than just lay out a series of historical
events and then combine them to form an understandable
story of what occurred. Good historians want to prove a
point, to show that a series of historical events mean one
thing rather than another. A history of the rise of Adolf
Hitler won't merely tell you that the National Socialist
Party, which he led, increased the number of its representatives in the German Reichstag (parliament) from 12 to
107 in the elections of 1930. It will attempt to describe the
conditions that led to such an outcome and to explain the
impact of the election on later events. Perhaps the author
will discuss unemployment, German nationalism, the car-
telization of German industry, the Treaty of Versailles, the
growth of the German Communist Party, anti-Semitism,
the structure of the German family, the philosophy of Nietz-
sche, or the insecurity of the lower middle class. The
author will probably deal with some of these more exten-
sively than others, and will attempt to show how the emphasized factors offer a better explanation of the subject
than any others. Although almost all historians will agree
on the number of National Socialist members of the 1930
Reichstag, each will construct the causes and effects of
that fact in different ways—sometimes in *very* different
ways. If you wish to understand a particular author's interpretation of an event, you must know how the author arrived at that interpretation and what significance he or she
believes it to have. Only a careful reading of the entire
work and close attention to the book's main arguments can
give you such knowledge. Remember, history books are a
selection of certain facts and interpretations constructed to
explain a particular writer's understanding of a historical
subject. If your own research relies heavily on a particular
book, you will need to know its theme and bias.

### Taking Notes
The first rule in note taking is to know in advance what
you are looking for. In order to avoid either taking note
after note that you will never need, or failing to note
things that you will, you should have a clear understanding of your topic and the kind of evidence you are seeking.

This is especially difficult at the outset of your research when your understanding of your topic is still somewhat vague. It is thus important to define the scope and content of your topic as quickly as possible or your research and note taking will wander, and valuable time will be lost.

As you go through a book, you will find portions that you will want to refer to in your own research paper. You will want to note the author's general idea or perhaps even record the actual words used. If you wish to quote, be careful to copy exactly the words in the book. Be sure that the meaning of the words you quote is clear and that you have not altered the author's point by quoting it out of context. If you wish to use a quotation, say, to show that Robert E. Lee was a good military strategist, a quotation such as "Lee was more admired by the average soldier than any other commanding officer" doesn't make that point because it refers to his popularity, not his generalship. Moreover, if the following sentence in the book is "However, his strategic decisions were not usually equal to those of Union army commanders," then you have actually altered the author's point by taking it out of its original context. Make sure you understand the author's meaning before you use a quotation. Also, be sure not to overquote. Do not quote more material than is necessary to convey the desired point clearly and accurately. Finally, never quote something simply because you find it difficult to express it in your own words. You will have to compose the idea in your own words when you write your paper, and it is best to think about the meaning of your research material now.

The most important points made by an author usually cannot be summed up in easily quotable form. When you want to record general arguments and conclusions, it is best to write your own paraphrase or summary of particular points. If the author has spent several pages relating the decline in trade between Spain and Mexico to the Wars of Mexican Independence, you may want to summarize the findings by noting that the author feels that the diminishing economic tie between colony and mother country was one of the major factors leading to Mexican independence. If you wish to note the evidence itself, you

may want to paraphrase the author's description of the decline in trade with several sentences of your own that include the main factors of this decline.

Whether you are quoting an author's exact words or
summarizing a point, the rules of note taking are the
same. As you read it is best to have a pile of index cards
beside you (4″ x 6″ or 5″ x 8″ are usually best). When you
come to something you want to note, write the author's
name, the book title, and the page number or numbers at
the top of the card.[3] The exact page numbers are essential
because you will have to use them when you write your
footnotes. If your quote or paraphrase covers more than
one page from your source, be sure to make that fact clear
on your note card. Also, it is essential to place each paraphrase or quotation on a separate card so that you can
arrange them by date or topic when you prepare your
paper. Placing a brief topic heading in the corner of each
card will make such arrangement easier. (See examples of
note cards on page 67.)

If you are quoting, be sure to use quotation marks and to
copy the quotation word for word. If you are quoting
something that the author has quoted, you must be sure to
point this out when you use the material and to identify
the original source. Be sure to include in your note an
introduction to the quoted material in your own words
stating who said it (if other than the author) and in what
context. This will insure that you use it properly in your
paper. If a quotation is very long and if there are parts that
relate to matters other than the one you are referring to,
then you may omit portions of the original quote by inserting ellipses, three periods ( . . . ), in the quoted material.[4]
For example, if the quotation reads "Feudalism, despite
later idealizations of it, was maintained by an oppressive
social order," you may want to leave out "despite the

[3]If you are taking notes on a journal or newspaper article, you will need
to record such information as date, volume number, page, and column
number.
[4]If the portion omitted is the end of a sentence, this is indicated by
inserting four periods—three to indicate omission and the fourth to indicate the end of the original sentence. In this case, the closing quotation
mark appears after the fourth period.

later idealizations of it," and quote the sentence as "Feudalism . . . was maintained by an oppressive social order." However, never omit anything if that would change the meaning of the material. If the sentence had read "Feudalism in its later stages in Moravia was maintained by an oppressive social order," the entire sentence would have to be quoted, or its meaning would be seriously altered.

To give a clearer sense of what note taking involves, here are two sample note cards. The first contains a quotation from a book and the second a paraphrasing of several paragraphs from an article.

## Sample Note Cards

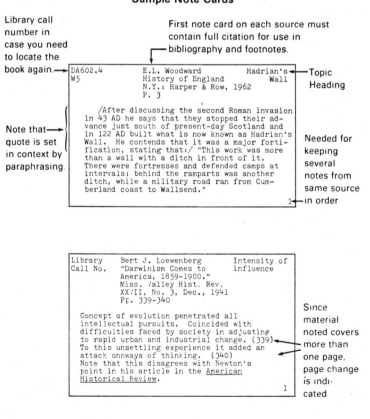

Library call number in case you need to locate the book again.

First note card on each source must contain full citation for use in bibliography and footnotes.

Topic Heading

Note that quote is set in context by paraphrasing

Needed for keeping several notes from same source in order

DA602.4 W5

E.L. Woodward Hadrian's
History of England Wall
N.Y.: Harper & Row, 1962
P. 3

/After discussing the second Roman invasion in 43 AD he says that they stopped their advance just south of present-day Scotland and in 122 AD built what is now known as Hadrian's Wall. He contends that it was a major fortification, stating that:/ "This work was more than a wall with a ditch in front of it. There were fortresses and defended camps at intervals; behind the ramparts was another ditch, while a military road ran from Cumberland coast to Wallsend."

Library Call No.

Bert J. Loewenberg Intensity of
"Darwinism Comes to influence
America, 1859-1900."
Miss. Valley Hist. Rev.
XXVII, No. 3, Dec., 1941
Pp. 339-340

Concept of evolution penetrated all intellectual pursuits. Coincided with difficulties faced by society in adjusting to rapid urban and industrial change. (339) To this unsettling experience it added an attack onnways of thinking. (340) Note that this disagrees with Newton's point in his article in the American Historical Review.

Since material noted covers more than one page, page change is indicated.

### Avoiding Plagiarism

The only thing worse than misquoting from your sources is plagiarizing from them. Plagiarism is easy to fall into. Because of your inexperience with your subject, it will be tempting to use the more sophisticated language of the historians you are reading. In most cases, their expertise will enable them to make their point clearly, and it is easy to get into the habit of using their words instead of your own. Don't fall into this trap. First of all, your instructor is also a historian and can tell the difference between the language of someone who has spent years researching a topic and that of the average history student. Second, and more important, is the fact that thinking is learning. If you substitute the simple task of copying for the more difficult but rewarding one of thinking about something and then putting it into your own words, then you are doing yourself a disservice.

To help you avoid plagiarism, here is a passage from J. Joseph Hutchmaker and Warren I. Sussman, eds., *Wilson's Diplomacy: An International Symposium* (Cambridge, Mass.: Schenckman, 1973), p. 13, followed by two paraphrasings. Paraphrase *a* constitutes plagiarism, but *b* does not. The subject is the diplomacy of Woodrow Wilson. Here is the original text:

> Wilson took personal responsibility for the conduct of the important diplomacy of the United States chiefly because he believed that it was wise, right, and necessary for him to do so. Believing as he did that the people had temporarily vested their sovereignty in foreign affairs in him, he could not delegate responsibility in this field to any individual. His scholarly training and self-disciplined habits of work made him so much more efficient than his advisers that he must have thought that the most economical way of doing important diplomatic business was for him to do it himself. Experience in dealing with subordinates who sometimes tried to defeat his purposes also led him to conclude

that it was the safest method, for he, and not his subordinates, bore the responsibility to the American people and to history for the consequences of his policies.

*Paraphrase a*

Wilson took personal responsibility for conducting diplomacy because he believed it was right for him to do so. Believing that the people had vested their sovereignty in foreign affairs in him, he couldn't delegate this responsibility. His scholarly training and self-discipline made him more efficient than his advisers. He thought that the most economical way of doing important business was to do it himself. Experience in dealing with subordinates who sometimes tried to defeat his purposes led him to conclude that it was the safest method because he bore responsibility to the American people for the consequences.

*Paraphrase b*

Wilson felt personally responsible for major diplomacy because he believed that the voters had entrusted him with such matters. He was more capable than his advisers in this area. He, and not his advisers, was responsible to the people.

Paraphrase *a* is too close to the original. Rather than recording the main points of the passage, it repeats many phrases word for word. Not only is it time consuming to take such lengthy notes, but the identical and almost identical phrases, if used as your own, would constitute plagiarism. The second paraphrase records only the principal point of the passage—that Wilson decided major foreign policy issues on his own because he felt personally responsible to the people in such matters. It does not copy the phraseology of the original. In this way, you save time, avoid plagiarism, and still are able to use the central idea of the passage. Paraphrasing that reduces your readings to their essential points and utilizes your own words is not easy at first. But mastering this technique will prevent plagiarism and produce a finished paper that is truly yours.

### Outlining and Organizing

When you have read all the sources on which you will base your own paper or presentation, you should have a series of index cards, each with a separate quotation, commentary, or summary of a point made, and each with the complete identification of the source from which it is taken.

In order to organize your notes, you need to make a tentative outline of your paper. If your topic is American blacks and the Depression, you may decide to deal with the topic chronologically and separate your paper into sections dealing with the period before 1929, the Hoover years, the early New Deal, and the late New Deal. Or perhaps you want to cover the subject topically, setting up separate sections on black reactions to economic discrimination, the National Association for the Advancement of Colored People, the U.S. Communist Party, organized labor, and New Deal legislation. Or perhaps you will want to consider the ideas of important black leaders and writers of the day, setting up sections dealing with E. Franklin Frazier, Richard Wright, Ralph Bunche, W. E. B. Du Bois, A. Philip Randolph, Langston Hughes, and Claude McKay.

A chronological approach begins with events that predate those that are the main focus of the paper. It then moves, step by step, through stages that group together spans of time. These spans may be in years, decades, or—for a very broad topic—centuries. Each time span is later than the one preceding it, and they generally do not overlap.

Time spans do not have to be the same length. It is best to use larger time units when discussing events that occurred long before the main events covered in the paper and to use smaller units when covering the period closest to the main events. A different rule applies to the length of each *section* of the paper: those portions dealing with periods removed from central events should be briefer than those portions close in time to such events.

A common problem with chronological organization is determining how far back in time to begin. Do you start ten or a hundred years before the time of the main events of the paper? A similar problem is determining where to stop. Do you stop with the main events themselves, or do you add sections covering later periods as well? There is no hard and fast rule, but it is wise not to cover too much ground. That is, don't start too long before or end too long after the principal events of your topic. A paper covering several hundred years is very unwieldy, and is best not handled by the chronological form of organization.

A topical form of organization is usually best for more general themes—those that deal with ideas, social systems, or other complex phenomena that involve a mixture of political, social, economic, cultural, and intellectual backgrounds. In this form of organization the task is not so much to build a historical sequence leading up to a particular event, but to weave a fabric composed of the many separate lines of historical development that form the background to the main topic. In many cases, the same topic can be organized by either method. If you have trouble choosing, or if you wish to explore other forms, your instructor should be able to help you.

To give you an idea of how a particular topic might be organized by each of the two methods, here are sample tables of contents of two papers called "The United States and the War in Vietnam."

*Chronologically:*
    Introduction
I.   The United States and the French War in Vietnam, 1946–1954
II.  The Geneva Conference of 1954
III. The Eisenhower Administration and the South Vietnamese Government of Ngo Dinh Diem, 1954–1960
IV.  Military Involvement Under President Kennedy, 1961–1963
V.   Escalation Under President Johnson, 1964–1968

    VI.     Negotiation and Troop Withdrawals Under President Nixon, 1060–1073
    VII.    Conclusion—The United States and Vietnam Today

*Topically:*
        Introduction
    I.      United States Economic and Political Interests in Vietnam
    II.     The History of Communism in Vietnam
    III.    United States Foreign Policy and Vietnam
    IV.    Congress and the War
    V.      The Antiwar Movement in the United States
    VI.     The Politics of the Republic of South Vietnam
    VII.    The Vietnam War and International Relations
        Conclusion

However you choose to organize your paper, you must organize your notes in the same manner. One of the best ways to do this is to read each of your note cards and mark it according to that part of the paper to which it applies. You may also want to describe briefly the contents of each card at the top. Then, when you prepare the final organization of your paper, you can arrange all your notes within each section according to the subjects to which they refer. (See section on organization, pages 78–80.)

### Budgeting Research Time

If you are writing, say, a fifteen- to thirty-page paper, expect to read about a dozen sources. This is not a firm figure, however, and your teacher and the subject you choose are better guides to the proper amount of research. If you read too few sources, your work will be shallow and perhaps unsatisfactory. If you read too many, you will not complete your work in the allotted time. It is best to make a tentative bibliography early in your research and discuss its adequacy in terms of topicality, authoritativeness, and length with your instructor. Discussion with your teacher of the preliminary outline for your paper should take place about this time also.

If you have never before written a long research paper,

you may be unsure as to how much time to allot to each aspect of your research and writing. Only experience will tell you the best budget of time for your particular work habits, but here are some general rules.

For a paper of fifteen to thirty pages due at the end of a fifteen-week semester, you should allow approximately 10 percent of your time (one to two weeks) for choosing a topic, preparing a tentative bibliography, and familiarizing yourself with the general contours of your topic; about 60 percent (seven to eight weeks) for reading the available research materials and taking notes from them; about 10 percent (another week) for thinking and talking about what you have read and organizing your notes; and about 20 percent (two to four weeks) for writing and typing the preliminary and final drafts.

If your term is much shorter than fifteen weeks, or if your assignment must be finished before the end of the semester, you will need to shorten your budget accordingly. (For a discussion of the preparation of papers of five to fifteen pages see Chapter 3.) Remember that by the end of the term exams will dominate your attention, and a paper due the final week of classes is best finished at least a week before that time so as not to conflict with studying for finals.

### Historical Materials Outside the Library

If you are fortunate, your topic will be one on which special historical materials are available at a nearby special collections library, a museum, a historical society, the archives of an institution or corporation, or film and audio tape libraries of television and radio studios.

Older members of your community or your own family also can be sources of historical information. People who have been leaders in local and national affairs have personal knowledge of important historical events. Perhaps you could prepare a series of questions concerning past events in which they were participants. You can write to these individuals, or perhaps speak with them. They may also have personal papers they would permit you to see. This kind of historical research is exciting and satisfying, and it may enable you to use primary historical material that no other historian has uncovered.

Elderly people are very good sources of historical material. They can tell of their years in another country or describe the America of fifty years ago in which they grew up. They may not have been important historical figures, but they reflect the experiences of countless others and are thus the stuff of which history is made. Their recollections of how they felt and of what they and others did and said when, for example, the *Titanic* sank, when Lindbergh flew across the Atlantic, or when Babe Ruth hit a record-breaking home run are priceless pieces of the historical puzzle.

### How to Research Your Family History

One of the most pleasurable kinds of historical research is the composition of your own family's history. Moreover, to do so is to recreate a portion of the historical experience of our nation. Because most of our ancestors came from other nations, a family history also will connect us with the historical experience of other lands. By studying the history of your family you become aware of your own place within these broader historical experiences. Perhaps most importantly, knowledge of your family's history and its meaning can give you a strong sense of your cultural roots that will strengthen you throughout your lifetime.

The best sources—and in many cases the only sources—of information on the history of your family are the recollections, understandings, and long-term possessions of your relatives. Researching a family history involves investigating these sources as thoroughly and creatively as possible. Rather than mastering the theme or weighing the evidence of a group of historical monographs or primary documents, research in this instance takes three forms: (1) familiarizing yourself with the general history of the nations and regions, and of the specific times and places, in which your ancestors lived; (2) studying all available family records, such as diaries, photographs, heirlooms; and finally, and most importantly, (3) interviewing all available family members.

The interview is the core of a family history because, in

most instances, it is the only way of uncovering the nature of your family's life. Without the recollections of your relations you would not be able to discover more than a handful of names, dates, and places—only the barest outline of your family's history.

In preparing for this crucial aspect of family research, you must familiarize yourself with the basic history of your family so that you can place in proper context the information you obtain from the people you interview. You will need to prepare your questions beforehand, focusing on important aspects of family life and of the larger social and political life surrounding the family. Be sure that your questions establish the basics: the names, relationships, and principal home and workplace activities of each member of the family in each generation, going as far down the trunk and out on the limbs of the family tree as possible given the scope of your project and the memories of your relatives. Keep away from trivia (your great-uncle's favorite dessert), and look for information that will enable you to make comparisons between generations of your family and between it and other families. Investigate such topics as the type of dwelling and neighborhood, parent-child and husband-wife relationships, authority and status patterns, income and social mobility. When you come across major family events—immigration, military service, job and residence changes, involvement in political movements—probe the reasons for them as they will illuminate the ties between your family and the nation's history.

In actually conducting the interview, use your prepared questions, taking care to make them as broad as possible; for example, "What was the neighborhood like when you lived there?" not "What was your address in 1936?" When you get an answer that seems to lead in the direction of important material, ignore your prepared questions temporarily and probe further. However, never interrupt an answer, even when the response seems unimportant. Your informants are the experts on their lives, and their self-perceptions—even if illogical or factually incorrect—are essential ingredients of family history. Finally, because the intricate web of your relative's feelings is as important as the milestones of his or her life, it is best to tape-record the interview if possible rather than rely on written notes. Record it all and then collect from your tapes the information which, on the one hand, best reflects your informants' testimony about their lives and, on the other, enables you to say something of importance about those lives and the times in which they were lived.

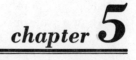

# chapter 5

# How to Write
# a Research Paper[1]

### The Theme

It is impossible to write a complete history of your subject, and you should not try. A good research paper will give the basic facts and interpretations concerning a subject, but it should not become a record of everything you have read. Your aim in writing a history research paper is to use your knowledge of the subject to develop a particular *theme*—a central point, assertion, or argument for the facts and interpretations of your paper. The goal of your writing should be to introduce the theme clearly, support it effectively, and then draw meaningful conclusions about it.

[1]This chapter contains generally accepted guides to writing style. Check to see if your instructor has any specific preferences which may vary from these.

Instead of merely describing the life of someone, the
course of a war, or the outcome of an election, your paper
should take a stand and make assertions. For example, a
paper on the siege of the Alamo should do more than tell
the story of the battle. It should make some central point
about the siege and argue its importance. Your instructor
will not be satisfied with a paper that describes the nature
of the fortifications, relates how many died, and concludes
that the defenders were very brave. You must find some
theme that explains the causes of the battle or that relates
the event to larger issues. Perhaps you will want to discuss
the morale of both forces and relate the course and outcome of the battle to the fighting ability of the Mexican
army or to the cause of Texas independence. If your subject is the early career of Chiang Kai-shek, instead of
merely relating the major events of his life, choose a
theme such as the effect of the Bolshevik Revolution on
his thinking or how his ideas on land reform influenced
his relationship with the Chinese Communist Party. With
your thematic focus, your facts and arguments become
relevant, and your paper develops them logically and
clearly.

### Organization

You can now break down your subject into those elements that best illustrate your theme. From your reading
you should be familiar with those aspects of it that were
given prominence, or that you yourself have concluded are
important. The outline of your paper should include sections that deal with these important areas in a way that
relates them to your theme. For example, if your subject is
the conflict between Israel and its Arab neighbors, your
research may have determined that two basic elements of
the subject are Zionism and Arab nationalism, and that two
important events were the Balfour Declaration of 1917 and
the United Nations Partition Plan of 1947. If most or all of
your sources mention these as important, then you must
find a place for them in your outline so that you will not
fail to cover them in your paper.

When a point is not stressed by your sources but you

have concluded that it is of significance to your theme, it should, of course, be included. For example, if your theme is Nasser's commitment to Arab nationalism and after researching the Arab-Israeli dispute you conclude that Nasser's reaction to his experiences in the war of 1948 was an important factor in his later conduct, then, even if your sources treated this matter very lightly, you will want it to appear in your outline.

When constructing an outline, be sure that you have enough facts to support each separate item. You cannot deal effectively with the issue of Nasser's experience in 1948 unless your notes contain evidence to support your point of view. Although you are free to draw your own conclusions from what you have read, your paper should not emphasize unsupported views you may have. If you feel very strongly about a particular point but don't find it supported by your research, then you must try to find some corroboration for your views. Even without support from other sources, however, you can still state your own opinions in your paper, but they should be clearly labeled as such.

In addition to pursuing your theme and covering the important points made in your reading, your outline should include an introduction and conclusion. The introduction should state the central theme and explain why you think the topic is important or interesting. The conclusion should sum up the major points, explain how they sustain your central theme, and discuss the importance of your theme for other subjects.

When constructing an outline, be sure that the sections are in a logical order. If you are treating your subject chronologically, each part of the outline must be in date order. If you are dividing your subject topically, each topic must raise a separate issue. Always keep in mind that the purpose of your outline is to develop your theme. If your subject is the role of the peasantry in the Mexican Revolution, and your theme is that the peasants' military role was crucial to the outcome of the Revolution, then the political philosophy of the liberal landowner Francisco Madero, regardless of its importance, should not be a part of your outline. Each part of the outline must pass two tests: does it relate to the theme, and does it deal with a different aspect of the theme from the other parts of the outline? (For sample outlines see pages 71–72.)

### Writing the Text

Once you have prepared your outline and separated your notes according to the parts of the outline to which they correspond, you will need to judge how long each section of the paper should be. The length and number of sections will vary according to the subject matter and the type of assignment, but here is a general guide: if your paper is to be about twenty-five pages long, it is best not to have more than six or seven sections. You will need at least three or four pages to treat adequately each of the points you want to cover. As you write each section, keep in mind the information you wish to include and the principal points you wish to develop. Form that section around the corresponding notes, making sure that you explain the relationships among the facts you present.

Your paper as a whole should contain an introduction, a central development (the body), and a conclusion. Likewise, each section should set out its particular point, move through the development of that point, and close with material that relates that point to those that follow. If your topic is German aid to the forces of General Francisco Franco in the Spanish Civil War, then the section that deals with the reasons behind German support might begin by briefly describing the circumstances surrounding Franco's appeal to Hitler in 1936. The main body of the section would explain in some detail Hitler's reasons for giving aid (for example, strategic and economic considerations, ideological and diplomatic factors) and would conclude by relating these reasons to the subject of later sections such as the actual aid given and its effect on the course of the war. Your principal concerns as you construct each section of your paper should be: does this section follow logically from the one preceding it; does it adequately support and develop the central theme; and does it establish the necessary background for the section that follows?

As each section mirrors the overall structure of the paper by containing an introduction, development, and conclusion, so each paragraph of which the section is composed contains a similar structure. A well-constructed paragraph begins with a sentence that introduces the information to be developed and concludes with a sentence that summarizes that information. If each paragraph is developed in this way, and if sentences explaining the relationship between paragraphs are included where necessary, then the paper as a whole becomes a tightly knit series of related statements rather than a random group of facts that do not seem to move in any clear direction. The key to tight construction is for each sentence to have two components: it must be related to the one preceding it, and it must continue the development of the theme to which it is related.

Here are two groups of sentences. The first is tightly constructed; the second is not.

In 1919, most Germans felt that the terms of the Versailles Treaty were harsh. In particular, they believed that the reparations and war-guilt clauses of the Treaty were unjust. When Hitler rose to power fourteen years later, he appealed to this sense of injustice in order to gain support for his program of denouncing the Treaty.

In 1919, most Germans felt that the terms of the Versailles Treaty were harsh. The French hoped to weaken German war-making capacity by forcing her to pay heavy war reparations. Hitler appealed to the German people to support his program to denounce the Treaty.

Despite the fact that each sentence in the second version is true, the paragraph does not hang together because the sentences are not clearly related. The first sentence refers to German feelings about the treaty, and then the second jumps to a discussion of French attitudes and drops the reference to the Versailles Treaty, which is the common theme that ties together the sentences of the first version. The third sentence further confuses the situation by jumping back to Germany and forward in time without any proper transition. On the other hand, the first version is tightly constructed because the second sentence, rather than breaking the line of development by bringing in a new element, expands and accentuates the point made in the first. The third sentence explains the forward jump in time and relates the events of the later period (Hitler's denunciation of the Treaty) to the German people's sense of injustice established in the first two sentences.

The best way to insure that there are no logical gaps between your sentences is to construct each paragraph from the viewpoint of the average person who might read your paper. Very often, a disconnected set of sentences may seem clear to you because as you write them you unconsciously fill in the gaps with your own knowledge. Your reader most likely does not have this knowledge and has to depend entirely on the words you write. If these are not enough to make your point clearly, you must be more explicit.[2]

It is often helpful to put your paper aside for a day or two and then reread it. By doing so, you can often gain a fresh perspective and can detect weaknesses that you hadn't noticed before.

### Example of Good Writing Style

The following is an example of a very well-written research paper. It appears here without footnotes or bibliography in order to focus your full attention on matters of organization and writing style. Rules and examples concerning footnotes and bibliography—both essentials of a good research paper—are discussed on subsequent pages.

To enable you to see the structure of this paper more clearly, the specific function of each group of sentences is indicated in the margin. Note that most sentences fall into one of three categories: (1) *developing the basic theme* set forth in the introduction, (2) giving *evidence* for or an *in-*

---

[2]The other basic component of clarity is a well-constructed sentence. No matter how well sentences are linked to one another, if the sentences themselves have faulty grammatical construction, the result will be unsatisfactory. If your sentence writing ability is weak, you should study one of the grammar and style manuals listed in Appendix B.

*terpretation* of a particular development of the theme, and (3) serving as a *transition* between two theme developments. The paper concludes with a summary of the theme's development and with the writer's own conclusions. Note that the subheadings serve both as statements of theme development and as transitions.

<u>The Impact of the Scientific Revolution</u>

<u>on Moral Philosophy</u>

<u>Introduction</u>

*(Statement of Theme)*

This paper shows how changes in knowledge lead to changes in social thought. It investigates the Scientific Revolution in Europe in the seventeenth and eighteenth centuries and the impact of that revolution on religious and moral thinking. The paper will try to show that the Scientific Revolution stimulated great changes in people's thinking about man, nature, and religion. However, scientific thought did not replace the older moral and religious teaching. Instead it combined with them to form new ideas.

<u>I. The Impact of the Scientific Revolution</u>

*(Thematic Development)*

The scientific discoveries of the seventeenth and eighteenth centuries in Europe were many, and they were fundamental to later scientific developments and to changes in social

*(Evidence)*

thought. These discoveries included the circulation of the blood by William Harvey, the properties of gases by Robert Boyle, the existence of microscopic organisms by Anton van

Leeuwenhoek, and the nature of combustion by
Antoine Lavoisier.  While the origins of these

discoveries can be found in the work of Greek
thinkers, Arab mathematicians, and medieval and
Renaissance philosophers, they were more than a
continuation of earlier work.  These discoveries
not only added new knowledge, they were the
products of innovative ways of thinking, such as
new theories of the nature of matter and of the

universe.  The effects of these new ways of
thinking were strongest in the fields of astronomy
and mechanics, where earlier conceptions of the
structure of the universe underwent a revolution.
The principal developments in these fields were
found in the work of Galileo Galilei in the
seventeenth century and Isaac Newton in the
eighteenth.

Early in the seventeenth century, Galileo
used the newly developed telescope to explore the
skies and make observations which proved that the
Copernican conception of the solar system was
correct.  Copernicus believed that the planets
revolved around the sun.  This challenged the
view of Ptolemy from ancient times, who held that
the earth was the center of the universe.  Thus,
the Copernican view relegated the earth to the
same status as all other heavenly bodies.  No
longer could it be held, as it had been by all
philosophers since Aristotle, that the movement of
earthly objects was completely different from

Evidence

those in space. Galileo's further experiments on moving bodies made clear that we can study objects on earth scientifically just as we can those in space. If mathematic regularity can

Interpretation

be applied to the movement of natural forces on earth as well as to those on other planets, then science could explain acts of nature and answer problems in engineering. This new way of viewing the universe would thus affect a wide range of human concerns.

Evidence

The discoveries of Isaac Newton were even more revolutionary. He developed a mathematical explanation for the motion of all bodies and called it the law of gravitation. This law stated that all matter is mutually attracting. Newton was even able to calculate precisely the intensity of the attraction because he discovered that it depended upon the mass of the bodies and their distance from one another. Now it could clearly

Interpretation

be demonstrated that stars and grains of sand were governed by the same laws. In Newton's view of the universe, the motion of all objects could be explained and even predicted. The universe was a giant machine run by physical laws. This meant that there was no room for religious explanations of how the universe worked. Thus it appeared that

Trans

the new science would challenge all Greek and Christian thought.

Thematic Dev

The new developments in astronomy and mechanics established the basis for modern experimental science. In the late seventeenth century, societies for the scientific study of nature grew up in many parts of Europe. Such groups as the Royal Society of London for Promoting Natural Knowledge spread the new thought and conducted experiments. They were part of a new secular outlook that challenged the religious beliefs of Europe. The new and the old explanations of the world seemed headed for inevitable conflict in their attempts to win the minds of people. What were the essential differences between these two world views and what was the outcome of their struggle?

## II.  Science Versus the Church

The new scientific and the old theological views of the universe seemed mutually exclusive. Christianity, through Scripture and other revelation, had an elaborate understanding of the divine origin of the world and of human beings and of the ways in which divine intervention ruled history. Alternative explanations were regarded as the product of ignorance of church teaching or as the work of the devil. On the other hand, science (or natural philosophy as it was then called) held that mathematical logic and tested experience (experimentation) were the only ways to discover truth. Any understanding of the world that was the result of religious experience or church authority was the product of superstition. Newtonian mechanics described a system in which all matter acted according to predictable physical rules. There was no need or even room for God in such a system, and observation and experimentation uncovered no sign of His influence.

The Catholic Church of the seventeenth and eighteenth centuries, while it had to share power with secular rulers, was still strong both theologically and politically. In many areas it had the power to enforce its views. The scientists ran great risk if they used their new ideas and discoveries in ways that threatened religion. Galileo was prohibited by church

authorities in Rome from writing about or even discussing the religious implications of the Copernican view of heavenly motions. Eventually, the Inquisition forced him to renounce the theory publicly, and his book on the subject, Dialogue on the Two Chief Systems of the World, was banned.

The disciplinary authority of the church (and of those governments influenced by it) was augmented by the fact that many of the new scientists had been ardent believers in the Christian faith. Either because they feared the power of the church and conservative governments or because they wished, despite their discoveries, to retain their religious convictions, these men sought some kind of theoretical compromise.

Newton, for example, continued to believe in God. While the operation of his system required no divine presence, he strongly believed that only God could have been the creator of such a mechanically perfect universe. As a result of these factors, the theoretical clash between science and religion was somewhat muted.

### III.  The Evolution of Scientific Thought:  Deism

One of the most widespread ideas among the new thinkers was a view that combined the new scientific understanding with a belief, however limited, in God. This idea was known as deism. Deists believed in a "natural religion," one that people arrived at by reason rather than faith. Since it was not reasonable that the universe created itself, men like John Locke, Samuel Clarke, and John Toland held that God was its creator. While He did not actually intervene once He had set the great machine in motion, God had initially endowed human beings with reason and moral sensibility. By using these faculties, people could learn both to understand nature and to build moral communities.

There were, of course, still major differences between Christianity and deism, and the deists were strong critics of the established church. They dispensed with the particulars of orthodox Christianity because these were the result not of reason but of superstition. The hierarchy of the church was also unnecessary since if all people could reason, all could come to an understanding of God on their own.

Nevertheless, deists did believe that the truths uncovered by scientific reasoning were the handiwork of the "Divine Architect."

IV.  The Evolution of Scientific Thought: Empiricism

Thematic Dev.

Other natural philosophers found the deist compromise unacceptable. These men tended to become agnostics or atheists. Some of these

Evid and Interp

skeptics held that if mechanical laws explained all things, then they also explained people's belief in God. What believers had taken as miracles, these men explained either as figments of the imagination or else as misunderstood natural phenomena such as earthquakes or lightning. If the evidence of God's presence was unfounded, they held, then there was no reason to assume His existence.

Thematic Dev.

Certain of these skeptics extended the material explanation of things to the workings of

Evid and Interp

the human mind. The philosophy of the British empiricists, in particular, maintained that the mind had no thought content of its own. It merely received sensory information and then made logical connections among the things observed. Since the world is governed by material laws, the impressions that reality makes upon the mind are regular and logical. To perceive truth, all one has to do is observe. If people believe in God, it is because their minds have been filled with superstitious notions which get in the way of understanding the truth as recorded by the senses. This school of empiricism believed that if people were taught to reason from nature rather than from authority, all could come to understand material reality, which was all there was to know.

Empiricism was a radical doctrine because it held that all people were capable of understanding the whole of reality and did not need to depend upon political or religious leaders to guide them.

Even more radical were those thinkers who were complete materialists and who not only explained thought as material in origin but also described human beings as just another piece of matter, with no different or higher properties. To these thinkers, if the mind merely registers sensory impressions, then it, too, is nothing more than a machine. Such materialist philosophers as La Mettrie described people as nothing more than a material arrangement of bones, muscles and nerves. Human thought was merely a particular combination or arrangement of these material elements. This conception eliminated not only the need for God but for any system of morality. As a result, La Mettrie preached hedonism, the pursuit of pleasure for its own sake, as a completely acceptable way of life. This view of morality was supported indirectly by the reports of explorers who brought home from their

scientific expeditions stories about the unusual
social customs of far-off primitive peoples.
The conclusion drawn by many scientifically
minded persons was that morality was culturally
taught and, therefore, relative.

## V.  The Evolution of Scientific Thought:  Skepticism

Perhaps the end (or rather dead end) of the
empirical school of thought is to be found in the
theories of David Hume.  This Scottish skeptic

mounted an attack on both theology and science.
He rejected the deist compromise with its
acknowledgment of God as the originator of the
universe.  There was no way of knowing, Hume
maintained, that the universe is a machine or that
it had to have been created.  These are only
inferences derived from the regularity of its
operation.  But what evidence do we have of its
regularity?  Only the impressions of our senses.
Hume questioned the reliability of sensory
impressions, attacking the foundations of
empiricism itself.  He argued that we have no way
of being certain that the things we perceive are
real.  All we know is the perception itself.  If
we cannot know things which are outside our minds,
then the causal connections we make between
events (the rising and setting of the sun, the
bouncing ball) are only habitual connections.
Cause and effect is an unprovable assumption.

## VI.  The Return Toward Nonmaterial Thought

With the new science now as dependent upon faith (in sensory impressions) as the old religion, the ground was prepared for a reconciliation. This was accomplished by the work of Immanuel Kant and Jean Jacques Rousseau.

Kant's _Critique of Pure Reason_ established a new position from which to view the interaction of mind and material reality.  Kant held that there were two kinds of mental processes; one kind is observation via the senses, and the other is _a priori_.  _A priori_ is the innate ability of the mind to order and reflect upon sensory impressions.  While he agreed with Hume that we cannot know what is outside our minds, he contended that, because the ability of the mind to organize experience is consistent and universal, we can be certain that our thinking is real and that it is understandable to others. Paradoxically, while we cannot know external reality, we can know our minds.  If the contents of our minds are real, then all our thought, both rational and spiritual, is real.  Once

again, there is room for belief in the nonmaterial.

It was Rousseau who reintroduced the nonmaterial and, in a sense, religious element into philosophical thinking.  He did so by

treating people's sense of right and wrong not as the result of religious teaching but as a

Evid and
Interp

basic human impulse. He held that the mind could not only reason, it also could feel. People had real emotions--love, hate, fear, pleasure--they were not mental machines. To Rousseau, thinking and feeling were both essential human qualities and were bound to each other.

Evid and
Interp

Rousseau felt that some of people's strongest feelings were religious ones and that these were not inferior to the reasoning aspect of mind. Of course, religion for Rousseau was not that of the church with its elaborate rituals or that of the deists to whom God was nothing more than an expert watchmaker. Rousseau's God was present in all natural things, those untouched by the corrupting influence of organized religion or any aspect of modern civilization. Rousseau believed that the conscience of man--the least contaminated part of him--was the best guide to both scientific and moral truth.

## Conclusion

Transition

Rousseau brings us to a point where thought is free to trust itself and to be both scientific and moral. Unreasoning faith and faithlessness are both rejected.

Summary

We have seen how the initial clash between science and religion led some scientific thinkers to attempt a synthesis and led others into a godless and eventually purposeless world. Furthermore, we have traced scientific thinking

*Summary*

back toward acceptance of nonmaterial, nonrational
ways of thought. Thus the undermining of the

*Interpretation*

Christian world view by scientific thinking was
paralleled by an evolution of such thinking
itself and in ways that illuminated the enduring
strength of moral and religious thought.

*Interp and Conclusion*

We have come a long way from the contest
between Galileo and the church over the ideas of
Copernicus. Today most people combine acceptance
of the Copernican universe and much other
scientific knowledge with some kind of religious
or moral teaching. What seemed in the
seventeenth century as a life and death struggle
between contradictory ways of thought has turned
out to be a standoff and has led to ways of
thinking undreamt of by the original antagonists.

### Footnotes

*What to Footnote.* Footnotes give the source of the facts
and opinions that appear in your paper. If you quote, paraphrase, or summarize from your research materials, you
must say where the original information can be found.
This is done so that the reader can check the accuracy of
your statements, judge the bias and credibility of your
sources, and carry out research of his or her own. On occasion you may also want to use footnotes to make comments
that supplement or qualify statements in your text.

A question that always troubles students is which statements in a paper need to be footnoted. There are no hard and fast rules concerning the use of footnotes. A professional scholar's criteria will be different from those of a student or amateur researcher. For the student writing a fifteen- to thirty-page term paper, three types of statements should be documented: (1) direct quotations, (2) controversial facts or opinions, and (3) statements that directly support the main points made in the paper.

All direct quotations must be footnoted. Controversial facts or opinions are those that not all of your sources agree on. If you state that most slave masters in Mississippi were kind to their slaves, and you know from your research that there are authors who strongly dispute this, then you must footnote that statement. A fact or opinion is also controversial if it is something with which the average reader would disagree. For example, you may have found that all your sources agree that Vikings visited the New World long before Columbus. However, if most people believe that Columbus was the first European to see the New World, then it is necessary to show your reader the source of your information with a footnote. Finally, statements of fact or opinion that directly support main points should be footnoted. If your subject is the Protestant Reformation, and you treat nationalism as a major factor in the break with Catholicism, then your references in the text to nationalist forces should be footnoted. On the other hand, if you treat the wealth of the Catholic Church as a very minor factor, then your references to that need not be footnoted.

The number of footnotes to use is another thorny problem. Some papers have more factual or controversial material than others and thus need more footnotes. As a rule of thumb, if your paper has quite a few pages without any footnotes, then you are probably not documenting as much as you should. On the other hand, if you are writing five or more footnotes per page, you may be overdoing it. There is no such thing as the *right* number of footnotes, but a twenty-five page paper might contain anywhere from fifteen to seventy-five footnotes, depending on the subject.

*How to Write Footnotes.* When you decide that a footnote is necessary, place a number at the end of the sentence that contains the information to be documented. Oc-
casionally, you may want to footnote two different things
in the same sentence. In this case, place each number
right after the word or phrase you want to footnote. Some
writers place the number at the end of a paragraph rather
than at the end of a sentence. This is proper only if the
footnote refers to the material in the paragraph as a whole.
If you are footnoting specific facts or quotations, the number should appear just after the facts or quoted material. If
you are footnoting a general idea or opinion, place the
number at the end of the paragraph or paragraphs that
discuss it. All footnote numbers should be placed a half
space above the line of typing. The number should not be
put in parentheses and should be inserted after any punc-
tuation (except a dash).

Some writers put their footnotes at the bottom of the
page. This is the form used in many of the books you will
use in your research. It is easier for the reader, but it
creates problems for the typist, who must judge how much
space to leave at the bottom of the page. An easier form,
and one that is acceptable to most instructors, is to put all
the footnotes at the end of the paper. If you use this
method, you must number your footnotes consecutively
throughout the work and write them on a separate piece of
paper as you compose the rough draft.

*Footnote Form.* The footnote form illustrated here is a
simplified one geared to beginning students.[3] If you have
sources that do not fit into these rules, you can check a
more advanced manual such as Kate L. Turabian, *Student
Guide for Writing College Papers* (Chicago: University of
Chicago Press, 1969). There are two basic forms for writing footnotes, one for books and one for articles:

    *Books*
        Crane Brinton, <u>A Decade of Revolution 1789–</u>

---

[3]Check to see if your instructor prefers a different form. Some do not
require publication information in footnotes.

1799 (New York: Harper and Brothers, 1934), pp. 18–22.
1. Author's name in full, followed by a comma.
2. Title in full, underlined.
3. Publication information (enclosed in parentheses and followed by a comma): place of publication, followed by a colon; name of publisher, followed by a comma; date of publication.
4. Page or pages cited, followed by a period.

Some book footnotes are more complex. If a book has several authors, or if it has a translator or editor, or was published in several volumes or editions, then the footnote has to include such information. For example:

T. W. Wallbank and A. M. Taylor, Civilization Past and Present, 2 vols., rev. ed. (Chicago: Scott, Foresman, 1954), 2:12, 104–117.

Note that when there are two authors, both are listed. If there are more than three authors, the footnote includes the name of the one listed first in the book followed by "et al." (and others). If there is more than one volume to a work, the total number of volumes must be specified and inserted after the title. The number of the specific volume used is placed before the page numbers and is separated from them by a colon. If the particular book used is a later edition of the work, that too is inserted after the title. Note also from the example that pages from two different parts of the same book can be covered in one footnote. If there is an editor or translator, that person's name, followed by "ed." or "trans." appears in the place reserved for the author's name:

Eugene C. Black, ed., Posture of Europe 1815–1940 (Homewood, Ill.: Dorsey Press, 1964), p. 102.

*Articles*

Dana F. Fleming, "The Role of the Senate in Treaty Making," American Political Science Review, XXVIII (August 1934), p. 583.

1. Author's name in full, followed by a comma.

2. Title of article, followed by a comma, all in quotation marks.
3. Title of periodical (journal or magazine), underlined and followed by a comma.
4. Volume number, date in parentheses, followed by a comma.
5. Page or pages cited, followed by a period.

If the article is an editorial or has no author, the footnote begins with the name of the article:

"America's Interest in the Cuban Economy," Barrons, XVI (January 20, 1936), p. 9.

This form is common for popular magazines, editorials, and many newspaper articles.

For specialized sources such as unpublished materials, book reviews, microfilm, speeches, dissertations, interviews, government documents, private correspondence, and radio or television programs, see a more specialized book, such as Turabian.[4]

A final rule about footnotes regards *second references* to the same source. If you refer to a particular book or article in more than one footnote, only the first reference has to have all of the information. The second reference to the *same* book need include only the author's last name and the page number.[5] If your first footnote read

Robert F. Kennedy, Thirteen Days (New York: W. W. Norton & Co., 1969), p. 14.

your second and later references would read simply

Kennedy, p. 123.
Kennedy, p. 168.

If, however, you are also referring to other books or articles by Robert Kennedy, you will have to repeat the title so your reader knows to which material you are referring.

The second time you refer to an article, you need to

---

[4]For a common list of abbreviations used in footnotes see Appendix B.
[5]Some instructors prefer second references to include a shortened title as well as the author's last name and the page number.

repeat only the name of the author and the page.[6] Thus if your first footnote to an article read

> Julius W. Pratt, "American Business and the Spanish-American War," Hispanic American Historical Review, XIV (May 1934), pp. 184–187.

your second and later references would read simply

> Pratt, pp. 189–191.

Again, if you are also referring to another article or book by Pratt, later references will have to include the name of the book or article.

Whenever you write a footnote, ask yourself: is it clear to the reader exactly which source I am referring to, and does that reader have enough information to find that source if necessary?

Here is a sample series of footnotes illustrating the various rules discussed above:

> [1]Charles Stanforth, *The Study of History* (New York: Crown, 1961), pp. 42, 122–127.
> [2]Cleveland Roland, "Machiavelli and Modern History," *Journal of the Philosophy of History,* XIV (February 1949), p. 49.
> [3]*Encyclopedia of Historical Science,* 2nd ed., "Whig Interpretation of History," by Rudolph Klein.
> [4]*Encyclopedia of Historical Science,* "Calvinism," by Nancy Ring Brenner.
> [5]Charles Stanforth, *Cyclical Theory in Arnold Toynbee* (London: Greath & Sons, 1950), p. 42. This view is also held, though less dogmatically, by Norman Parton, *Ancient and Modern Thinking* (London: Fernival & Ashwood, 1956), pp. 98–106.
> [6]"Historians at War Again," *Los Angeles Dispatch,* January 14, 1969, sec. B, p. 2.
> [7]Michelle Arnold and Dana Swope, eds., *New Trends in Historiography* (Philadelphia: Claxton, 1972), p. 104.
> [8]Stanforth, *Cyclical Theory,* p. 14.
> [9]Roland, p. 50.

Explanation of footnote citations:

Footnote 1: Book; first citation.

2: Article; first citation.

3: Reference work. Author and pub-

[6]See footnote 5.

lisher not needed; edition or date of publication is needed; title and author (if mentioned) of article consulted; volume and page number not needed because of alphabetical arrangement of work.

4: Reference work; second citation but to different article.

5: Book; first citation (even though author was previously mentioned in footnote 1). Note that you can refer to more than one source in a footnote as long as you explain your reason for doing so.

6: Newspaper article.

7: Book; multiple authors or editors.

8: Book; second citation. Short title needed because two different works by this author were previously cited.

9: Article; second citation. No short title needed because no other work by this author is cited.

### Quotations

*What to Quote.* Don't quote too often, and don't make quotations too long. Many students tend to rely on other people's words more than necessary. Unless the exact words of your source are crucial to making an important point, or unless great controversy surrounds the statement, it is not necessary to use a quotation. In most cases a paraphrase or summary of the statement, properly footnoted, is sufficient. If you do quote, be sure to quote enough of the original statement to make its meaning clear, but do not make the quotation any longer than necessary. Remember that a quotation must clearly be labeled as such and the speaker clearly identified.

*Quotation Form.* If a quotation is brief, taking up no more than two or three lines of your paper, then it should be written as a part of the text and surrounded by quotation marks. You should introduce the quotation with a clear identification of the speaker. If you do not wish to quote a whole statement, it is necessary to indicate those parts you are leaving out by inserting ellipses. (See example on pages 66–67.)

If your quotation is very long it must be separated from the sentences that precede and follow it. It should be indented ten or more spaces and appear in single-spaced type. Do not surround it with quotation marks.

*Short quotation example:*
The early settlers were not hostile to the Indians. As pointed out by the Claxton *Banner* in 1836: "Our Sioux neighbors, despite their fierce reputation, are a friendly and peaceable people."

*Short quotation example with omission:*
As pointed out by the Claxton *Banner* in 1836: "Our Sioux neighbors . . . are a friendly and peaceable people."

*Long quotation example:*
The early settlers were not hostile to the Indians. As pointed out by the Claxton *Banner* in 1836:
Our Sioux neighbors, despite their fierce reputation, are a friendly and peaceable people. No livestock have been disturbed, and the outermost cabins are unmolested. We trust in God that our two peoples may live in harmony in this territory.

It is also possible to insert quoted material in the middle of a sentence (for example, the Prime Minister favored the proposal, but the Foreign Secretary felt it to be "a most dangerous course to pursue," and urged its rejection). In most cases like this, however, a paraphrase is preferable to a quotation. (The Prime Minister favored the proposal, but the Foreign Secretary considered it dangerous and urged its rejection.) Whether you choose to quote or paraphrase, all such references must be footnoted.[7]

[7]If a portion of the material you are quoting is in italics (e.g., *New York Times*), you should underline these words when you type them (e.g., New York Times).

### Organizing a Bibliography

A bibliography is a listing of the sources you used in writing your paper.[8] The list should appear on a separate page or pages at the end of the paper. If the bibliography is long, say more than twenty sources, it should be divided into three categories: (1) primary sources and documents, (2) books, and (3) articles. The sources are listed alphabetically according to the last name of the author. The form for a book is

> Link, Arthur S. <u>Woodrow Wilson and the Progressive Era</u>. New York: Harper and Row, 1954.

1. Author, last name first, followed by a period.
2. Title of work, underlined, followed by a period.
3. Place of publication, followed by a colon.
4. Publisher, followed by a comma.
5. Date of publication, followed by a period.

The form for articles is

> Bettman, Irwin. "The Beet Sugar Industry: A Study in Tariff Protection." <u>Harvard Business Review</u>. XI (April 1933), pp. 369–378.

1. Author, last name first, followed by a period.
2. Title of article, followed by a period, all in quotation marks.
3. Name of the periodical, underlined, followed by a period.
4. Volume number, followed by date in parentheses, followed by a comma.
5. Pages on which the article begins and ends, followed by a period.

If there is more than one author, the citation is alphabetized according to the last name of the first author mentioned on the title page of the work. That name is then followed by *all* the others, again with last names first. If there is more than one work by a particular author, only

---

[8]It must include all those sources that appear in footnotes. You need not list every source you looked at in the course of your research. Don't pad the bibliography just to make it look more impressive.

the first listing in the bibliography carries the author's name. All the rest begin with an eight-space underline in place of the name. As with footnotes, if the author is the translator or editor, or if there is more than one volume, these must be noted. If a book is anonymous, it is listed in alphabetical order, by its title. If an article has no author, it is listed, in alphabetical order, by the title of the article. If you have used many volumes of a particular periodical or many issues of a particular newspaper, you need not list each one separately in your bibliography. They should appear, listed by the name of the periodical or newspaper, as follows:

Monthly Labor Review. Vols. XL–LXX. Washington: United States Bureau of Labor Statistics, 1940–1957. New York Times. 1954–1958.

The rules governing bibliographical citations for primary documents can be complicated. The best system is to copy the information exactly as it appears in the card catalog.

Here is a sample bibliography illustrating the rules discussed above. It is drawn from the series of footnotes appearing on page 99.

Arnold, Michelle and Swope, Dana, eds. *New Trends in Historiography.* Philadelphia: Claxton, 1972.
*Encyclopedia of Historical Science,* 2nd ed. "Calvinism" by Nancy Ring Brenner.
————. "Whig Interpretation of History" by Rudolph Klein.
"Historians at War Again." *Los Angeles Dispatch,* January 14, 1969.
Parton, Norman. *Ancient and Modern Thinking.* London: Fernival & Ashwood, 1956.
Roland, Cleveland. "Machiavelli and Modern History." *Journal of the Philosophy of History.* XIV (February 1949), 46–60.
Stanforth, Charles. *Cyclical Theory in Arnold Toynbee.* London: Greath & Sons, 1950.
————. *The Study of History.* New York: Crown, 1961.

### Revising and Rewriting

Leave time for revising your paper. The process of putting together the research and writing of a history paper is complex, and your first draft will need smoothing out. As you prepare the final draft, check your paper for the following: (1) Does the paper have thematic unity and do its parts follow one from the other? (2) Is there adequate support for the major assertions of fact and interpretation? (3) Are the points made clearly and forcefully? You must also check the mechanics of your paper, especially spelling and grammar. If your paper is typewritten, check for typographical errors, and make all corrections cleanly and clearly. Reading the paper aloud will help you to catch poor sentence construction and awkward phrases.

Preparing your final draft also involves knowledge of the rules of typing style. Make sure that all pages are numbered consecutively, that the sections or chapters are clearly delineated, and that the footnotes and bibliography are clearly separated from the text and neatly organized. If your paper contains additional material such as appendices, graphs, charts, drawings, photographs, or maps, these too must be clearly labeled and separated from the text. If there are many such materials, your paper should contain a table of contents that lists them. Last of all, choose a title for your paper—one that clearly and accurately reflects its contents.

### Typing Form

Choose a medium- or heavy-weight paper for your final copy. It is wise to make a copy of your work in case part or all of the original is lost. Leave at least an inch margin on all sides. (Sometimes an inch and a half on the left margin is preferable.) Double-space the text except for long quotations and footnotes. Give each page a consecutive number in the upper right-hand corner. Prepare a separate title page that includes the title (underlined) and your full name. Also include any information that may be needed to identify the work, such as the name and number of the course, the day and time of meeting or section number, the instructor's name, and the date. Check with your instructor for specific instructions.

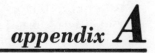
# Basic Reference Sources for History Study and Research

This appendix can be used as a supplement to the reference collection of your school library.[1] To aid you in your research, the sources are separated according to the kind of information they contain and, where appropriate, they are organized according to area or subject. This should be of particular value in locating sources at the very beginning of your study of a particular subject. If you have no initial leads on relevant material, or if you are unsatisfied with the sources you have uncovered, the works listed here may enable you to find pertinent facts and historical works.

The reference sources cited here are especially designed for historical research. There are two kinds of works listed: reference books, which contain summary or

[1]For information on how to use reference sources in the library see pages 54–59.

statistical historical information, and bibliographies, which contain lists of historical works on particular periods or subjects. Reference books (dictionaries, encyclopedias, biography collections, etc.) are useful for obtaining specific facts or for organizing a general outline of your subject. Bibliographies do not themselves contain historical information but rather are collections of history works on a particular topic.

The purpose of this appendix is to facilitate your search for relevant historical facts and history books. Because it is organized with the needs of the beginning student in mind, it may be easier to use than the reference catalog in your school library. It is therefore a good place to *begin* your research. However, as stated before, it is meant as a *supplement* rather than as a substitute for your library's reference catalog. Many of the works cited here should be available in a good college or public library, but some of them, particularly the specialized bibliographies, may not be. If there is a book listed here that you feel is most valuable for your research and it is not in your library's reference catalog, you will have to try another library or find a comparable work that your library does possess. On the other hand, if your school or public library is a large one, there will be many more sources in its reference catalog than are listed in this chapter, and you should treat these listings as only a first step in your research.

Within each group of sources, those that should be found in most library reference collections or that are particularly useful to beginning students are designated by an asterisk (*). Those without the asterisk are works less likely to be available at smaller libraries and are generally designed for the use of advanced students and professionals. If any of the latter should be available, however, you may find them valuable in your research.

The books in this appendix are listed by title first so that you can easily sight the work that seems closest to your topic. Following the title is the publication information and then the name of the editor or compiler. When looking up these works in your school or public library's reference catalog, check first under the name of the editor or compiler. If the book is not listed there, it may be filed under the title of the work or possibly the publisher. Where there is more than one edition of a work, use the most recent one available.

## 1. DICTIONARIES, ENCYCLOPEDIAS, ATLASES, YEARBOOKS, ETC.

These books are general reference works. They can help you to define and correctly spell important terms, gather general information on a particular subject, locate geographical areas, obtain statistical data, and much more. These sources are a good point at which to begin any historical investigation or to consult for a specific fact. However, they do not contain serious developments or interpretations of historical subjects, and therefore should not be depended upon for the substance of your work.

### A. GENERAL DICTIONARIES

*Oxford English Dictionary*. Oxford: Clarendon Press, 1888–1928. James A. H. Murray et al., eds. "A New English Dictionary on Historical Principles." This is the most complete English-language dictionary. If you are studying the historical development of the meaning of a word, it is an essential reference. If, however, your concern is to determine the contemporary spelling or definition of a term, the following unabridged language dictionaries are better sources. If the term you are searching for is colloquial or is a recent derivation, be sure to use the most recent edition available.

*\*Webster's New International Dictionary*
*\*Funk and Wagnall's New Standard Dictionary*
*\*The Random House Dictionary of the American Language*

### B. HISTORICAL DICTIONARIES

These dictionaries define only historical terms. Unlike language dictionaries, they also give a brief description of the origin and general historical context of the term. Some have quite extensive explanations of historical terms and thus are similar to encyclopedias.

*Webster's Guide to American History.* Springfield, Mass.:
G. and C. Merriam, 1971.
*Concise Dictionary of American History.* New York:
Scribners, 1962. Thomas C. Cochran and Wayne An-
drews, eds.
An *Encyclopedic Dictionary of American History.* New
York: Washington Square Press, 1968. Howard Hur-
witz, ed.
*Dictionary of American History.* New York: Scribners,
1942–1961. James T. Adams and Roy V. Coleman eds.
(Revised edition, 1976.) This is the most extensive
dictionary of American history.
*Concise Dictionary of Ancient History.* New York: Philo-
sophical Society, 1955. Percival Woodcock, ed.
A *Dictionary of British History.* New York: St. Martin's
Press, 1970. Sigfrid H. Steinberg, ed.
A *Dictionary of Modern History, 1789–1945.* Baltimore:
Penguin Books, 1975. A. W. Palmer, ed.

C. SOCIAL SCIENCE DICTIONARIES

*Dictionary of Social Science.* Washington, D.C.: Public Affairs Press, 1959. John T. Zadrozny, ed.
*Dictionary of Social Sciences.* New York: The Free Press,
1964. J. Gould and W. Kolb, eds.

D. GENERAL ENCYCLOPEDIAS

*Encyclopaedia Britannica.* Chicago: Encyclopaedia Britannica Corporation, 1974. This is one of the best encyclopedias. If your subject is a recent one, or if important
new facts and interpretations have arisen in recent
years, be sure to obtain the latest edition of whatever
encyclopedia you use. If a recent edition is not available, check the annual supplements published by most
good encyclopedias.
*Encyclopedia Americana.* New York: The Americana
Corporation.
*Collier's Encyclopedia.* New York: Crowell Collier and
Macmillan.
*The Columbia Encyclopedia.* 4th ed. New York: Columbia
University Press, 1975.

E. HISTORICAL ENCYCLOPEDIAS

*An Encyclopedia of World History, Ancient, Medieval and Modern, Chronologically Arranged.* Boston: Houghton Mifflin, 1972. William L. Langer, ed.

*Harper Encyclopedia of the Modern World* [1760 to present]. New York: Harper & Row, 1970. Richard B. Morris and Graham W. Irwin, eds.

*Encyclopedia of American History.* New York: Harper & Row, 1976. Richard B. Morris, ed.

F. SOCIAL SCIENCE AND SPECIALIZED ENCYCLOPEDIAS

*International Encyclopedia of the Social Sciences.* New York: Macmillan, 1968. David L. Sills, ed. If your research takes you into such fields as political science, economics, anthropology, law, sociology, and psychology, this is an important source book for you. An earlier work, *Encyclopedia of the Social Sciences* (New York: Macmillan, 1930–1934), edited by Edwin R. A. Seligman and Alvin Johnson, is also valuable for such subjects, although it is now out of date.

*Encyclopedia of Philosophy.* New York: Macmillan, 1966. Paul Edwards, ed.

*The International Jewish Encyclopedia.* Englewood Cliffs, N.J.: Prentice-Hall, 1973. Ben Isaacson and Deborah Wigoder, eds.

*New Catholic Encyclopedia.* New York: McGraw-Hill, 1967.

G. GENERAL ATLASES

*The Times Atlas of the World.* London: Times Publishing Company, 1955–1959. John Bartholomew, ed. Vol. I— World, Australia, East Asia; Vol. II—India, Middle East, Russia; Vol. III—Northern Europe; Vol. IV— Mediterranean and Africa; Vol. V—Americas. A one-volume edition was published in 1971.

*Oxford Economic Atlas of the World.* Oxford: Oxford University Press, 1972.

*Webster's Geographical Dictionary.* Springfield Mass.: G. and C. Merriam. This source is not useful for map reference but is a convenient source for determining the spelling, location, and description of geographical terms.

*Oxford Atlas of the World.* New York: Oxford University Press, 1966.

*National Geographic Atlas of the World.* Washington, D.C.: National Geographic Society, 1970.

H. HISTORICAL ATLASES

*Shepherd's Historical Atlas.* New York: Barnes & Noble, 1964. William R. Shepherd, ed.

*Historical Atlas of World History.* Chicago: Rand McNally, 1965. Robert R. Palmer et al., eds.

*\*Historical Atlas of the United States.* New York: Henry Holt & Company, 1953. Clifford L. Lord and Elizabeth H. Lord, eds.

*Muir's Atlas of Ancient and Classical History.* New York: Barnes & Noble, 1961.

*\*Muir's Historical Atlas: Ancient, Medieval & Modern.* New York: Barnes & Noble, 1962.

*Atlas of European History.* New York: Oxford University Press, 1957. Edward W. Fox and H. S. Deighton, eds.

*Atlas of World History.* Chicago: Rand McNally, 1965. Robert R. Palmer et al., eds.

I. YEARBOOKS

*\*Statesman's Yearbook.* New York: Macmillan, 1864–present. This and the following yearbooks provide up-to-date political information, especially of a governmental nature.

*Political Handbook of the World.* New York: Harper & Row, 1927–present. Council on Foreign Relations. Walter H. Mallory, ed.

*United Nations Statistical Yearbook.* New York: United Nations Statistical Office, 1949–present. There is also a *United Nations Demographic Yearbook,* which provides world and national population statistics.

## 2. BIOGRAPHY COLLECTIONS

These works are collections of short biographies of well-known persons. They contain a general outline of the mile-

stones and accomplishments of individuals who are considered to have made notable contributions to the times
in which they lived and/or to posterity. These works are
useful as a first step in biographical research on persons
central to your topic or as a way of identifying characters
peripheral to it. Each collection has different criteria for
determining which individuals it includes. Take care to
select the biography collection that is most likely to include the type of individual on whom you are seeking
information.

A. GUIDES TO BIOGRAPHY COLLECTIONS

*Biography Index: A Cumulative Guide to Biographical
Material in Books and Magazines.* New York: H. W.
Wilson, 1949–present.
*Biographical Dictionaries: Master Index.* Detroit: Gale
Research, 1975.

B. BRITISH BIOGRAPHY COLLECTIONS

*Dictionary of National Biography.* Oxford: Oxford University Press, 1908–present. Leslie Stephen and Sid-
ney Lee, eds. Supplement, Boston: G. K. Hall, 1966.
*Who's Who.* London: Allen & Unwin, 1849–present. Annual. This volume covers *living* individuals. For historical research, you must choose a year during which
your subject was most active, or preferably use the
*Who Was Who* collection, which follows.
*Who Was Who.* Vol. I, 1897–1915; Vol. II, 1916–1928; Vol.
III, 1929–1940; Vol. IV, 1941–1950. (See annotation to
*Who Was Who in America* for further information.)

C. AMERICAN BIOGRAPHY COLLECTIONS

*Dictionary of American Biography.* New York: Scribners,
1928–1958, including supplements. This is the best
source for biographies of historical personages of the
United States. It includes both U.S. citizens and
people who lived much of their lives in this country
even if they were not citizens. It lists only individuals
who are no longer living. As with most biography collections, the date of original publication is the best

key to determining who is included. Most of these volumes were written between 1928 and 1936. If your subject died after 1928, check the supplements. Supplement I covers deaths through the end of 1935; supplement II, 1940; supplement III, 1945. A one-volume work containing shortened versions of these biographies was published in 1964 under the title *Concise Dictionary of American Biography.*

*National Cyclopedia of American Biography.* Ann Arbor, Mich.: University Microfilms, 1967. Unlike the *Dictionary of American Biography*, this is not an alphabetical listing, but it does have an alphabetical index at the end of each volume. This collection is published in two series: a "Current" series and a "Permanent" series. The Permanent series includes only individuals no longer living at date of publication for the volume in which they were to be included. Although this work was reprinted in 1967, the original volumes of the Permanent series were written in the 1890s. If your subject was living in the twentieth century, consult the Current series, which includes only persons living at date of publication.

*Who's Who in America.* Chicago: Marquis Who's Who, 1897–present. This volume covers living individuals. For purposes of historical research you must obtain the older volumes or, preferably, use the *Who Was Who* collections that follow.

*Who Was Who in America.* Vol. I, 1897–1942; Vol. II, 1943–1950; Vol. III, 1951–1960. Chicago: Marquis Who's Who, 1943, 1950, 1962. The years covered in each volume indicate the dates of death for those included. For example, if your subject died in 1945, he/she should be included in Vol. II. For individuals who died before 1897, see *Who Was Who in America: Historical Volume, 1607–1896.*

*\*Who Was Who in America: Historical Volume, 1607–1896.* Chicago: Marquis Who's Who, 1967.

*Biographical Directory of the American Congress, 1774–1971.* Washington, D.C.: Government Printing Office, 1971.

*Biographic Dictionary of the United States Executive, 1774–1977.* Westport, Conn.: Greenwood Press, 1977.

*Who's Who of American Women.* Chicago: Marquis Who's Who, 1973.

*Biographical Directory of American Labor Leaders.* Westport, Conn.: Greenwood Press, 1974. Gary M. Fink, ed.

*A Bibliography of American Autobiographies.* Madison: University of Wisconsin Press, 1961. Louis Kaplan et al., comps.

*American Men and Women of Science.* New York: Bowker, 1906–present.

*Directory of American Scholars.* New York: Bowker. American Council of Learned Societies.

D. INTERNATIONAL BIOGRAPHY COLLECTIONS

These collections list persons of all national origins.

*\*Current Biography.* New York: H. W. Wilson, 1940–present. This covers living persons. Older volumes, however, may list individuals who are now of historical significance. Only useful for historical research for the period since the 1930s. To locate the volume you need check *Current Biography: Cumulated Index, 1940–1970.*

*International Who's Who.* London: Europa, 1935–present.

*New York Times Obituary Index, 1858–1968.* New York: New York Times, 1970.

*Encyclopedia of World Biography.* New York: McGraw-Hill, 1973. David I. Eggenberger, ed.

*Chambers's Biographical Dictionary.* New York: St. Martin's Press, 1969. J. O. Thorne, ed.

E. NATIONAL BIOGRAPHY COLLECTIONS

Most national biography collections, except for the United Kingdom and the United States, which are covered separately, deal with contemporary personages. However, they may be useful for research into recent history or for obtaining information on the early careers of contemporary figures. Here is a brief selection.

*Dictionary of Canadian Biography.* Toronto: University of
   Toronto Press, 1966–present.
*Who's Who in Latin America.* Chicago: A. N. Marquis,
   1946–1951. Percy A. Martin, ed.
*Who's Who in Communist China.* Hong Kong: Union Re-
   search Institute, 1966.
*Who's Who in the Union of Soviet Socialist Republics.*
   New York: Scarecrow Press, 1966.
*Dictionary of African Biography.* New York: Reference
   Publications, 1977–present. Volumes expected on
   each African country.
*Southern African Dictionary of National Biography.* Lon-
   don: Warne, 1966. Eric Rosenthal, ed.
*Japan Biographical Encyclopedia and Who's Who.* Tokyo:
   Renzo Press, 1958–present.
*Biographical Dictionary of Republican China.* New York:
   Columbia University Press, 1967–1970.

F. SPECIALIZED BIOGRAPHY COLLECTIONS

*A Biographical Dictionary of World War II.* New York: St.
   Martin's Press, 1972. Christopher Tunney, ed.
*Dictionary of Scientific Biography.* New York: Scribners,
   1970–1976. Charles C. Gillispie, ed.
*Who's Who in Jewish History: After the Period of the Old
   Testament.* New York: McKay, 1974. Joan Comay, ed.

## 3. NEWSPAPER DIRECTORIES AND INDEXES

In most cases, the beginning student will have access
only to the few newspapers held in his or her school or
local public library. If you determine, however, that a particular newspaper is of special importance to you, the best
way to locate back issues is to check a newspaper directory. These directories can tell you in which libraries that
newspaper can be found and how complete the collection
is. Remember, the newspaper directory is of use only if
you know the name of the particular paper for which you
are looking. Moreover, unless you have easy access to a
large university or public library, most of the newspapers
in a directory will be located far from your school. You

might be able to obtain the newspapers you need if they are on microfilm, but this can take several weeks. In most cases, it is best to confine yourself to the newspaper collections in nearby libraries.

A. NEWSPAPER DIRECTORIES

*American Newspapers, 1821–1936: A Union List of Files Available in the United States and Canada.* New York: H. W. Wilson, 1937. Winifred Gerould, ed.

*Newspapers on Microfilm: A Union Check List.* Washington, D.C.: Library of Congress, 1963. George Schwegman, Jr., ed.

*African Newspapers in Selected American Libraries.* Washington, D.C.: Library of Congress, 1962.

*Latin American Newspapers in United States Libraries.* Austin: University of Texas Press, 1969. Steven M. Charno, ed.

B. NEWSPAPER INDEXES

Once you know that you have access to a particular newspaper, you must determine which issues contain articles on your subject. If your subject is a specific event, then merely check the issues of the newspaper published at the time or shortly after the event. However, if you are seeking articles about an event that was not confined to a particular day or week (for example, the stock market crash of 1929), then you will have to check newspaper issues covering many weeks or even months. An indispensable aid in such a task is the newspaper index.

If you know the year in which the event occurred, then a newspaper index can tell you the days in that year when a particular paper contained articles or editorials on your subject. Because the index saves you the trouble of reading each issue, it is indispensable for research into events that were not limited to a brief period. The only problem with newspaper indexes is that there are so few of them. If there is no index to the paper you wish to read, the best thing to do is to check the index of another newspaper. This will tell you the dates on which that newspaper carried articles on your subject. You can then go back to the newspaper in which you were initially interested and read it for those dates. In most cases you won't be far off.

*New York Times Index.* New York: New York Times, 1913–present. This is usually the best source for beginning students. Most libraries have files of the *New York Times*, and the index is very complete.

*New York Daily Tribune Index.* New York: Tribune Association, 1876–1907.

*Palmer's Index to The Times* [of London] *Newspaper*, 1790–1943. London: 1868–1943.

*Official Index to The Times* [of London]. London: 1907–present.

*Christian Science Monitor Index.* Corvallis, Oregon: 1960–present. Because it goes back only to 1960, it is of limited use for historical research.

## 4. PERIODICAL GUIDES AND INDEXES

Periodical guides describe the general content and location of periodicals. Like newspaper guides, they are most useful if you already know that you want a particular periodical and are seeking information as to where collections of it can be found. If the periodical guide lists no library convenient to you, it is best to check into other periodicals.

### A. PERIODICAL GUIDES

*Union List of Serials in Libraries of the United States and Canada.* New York: H. W. Wilson, 1943.

*New Serial Titles: A Union List of Serials Commencing Publication after December 31, 1949.* Washington, D.C.: Library of Congress, 1953–present. If you are seeking a newer periodical, this guide is the best source.

*Historical Periodicals: An Annotated World List of Historical and Related Serial Publications.* Santa Barbara, Cal.: ABC-Clio, 1961. Eric H. Boehm and Lalit Adolphus, eds.

*Guide to Current Latin American Periodicals.* Gainesville, Fla.: Kallman Publishing, 1961. Irene Zimmerman, ed.

B. GENERAL PERIODICAL INDEXES

These works list articles that have appeared in periodical publications. They are usually organized by subject and contain all of the articles on a given topic that appeared in the periodicals that are indexed. The periodicals covered by a particular index are usually listed at the very beginning of the volume. When you choose an index be sure that it covers the kind of periodical likely to contain articles on your subject and that these articles are written for a serious or scholarly audience.

*Historical Abstracts.* Santa Barbara, Cal.: ABC-Clio, 1955–present. Part A: Modern History (1450–1914); Part B: The Twentieth Century (1914–present). Eric H. Boehm, ed. This is the best source for articles in history journals. It covers a very wide range of subjects.

*Reader's Guide to Periodical Literature.* New York: H. W. Wilson, 1900–present. These volumes cover the twentieth century. You must be selective when using them because many of the periodicals they cover are written for a popular rather than a scholarly audience. However, the magazines listed are valuable as records of popular opinions and interests.

*Nineteenth Century Reader's Guide to Periodical Literature.* New York: H. W. Wilson, 1944.

Poole's Index to Periodical Literature, 1802–1881. Boston: Houghton Mifflin, 1891. There is a supplement covering 1882–1906.

*Social Science and Humanities Index.* New York: H. W. Wilson, 1907–1973. This is often the best single guide for historical researchers.

Social Science Index. New York: H. W. Wilson, 1974–present. For the period prior to 1974 see *Social Science and Humanities Index.*

Humanities Index. New York: H. W. Wilson, 1974–present. For the period prior to 1974 see *Social Science and Humanities Index.*

*Public Affairs Information Service Bulletin.* New York: P.A.I.S., 1915–present. This work emphasizes periodicals and other publications in the social sciences and includes many government publications.

C. SPECIALIZED PERIODICAL INDEXES

There are many periodical indexes on specialized topics. If your research takes you into these specialized fields, the indexes listed here may be worth looking into.

*Agricultural Index; Applied Science and Technology Index; Art Index; Business Periodicals Index; Education Index; Index to Legal Periodicals; Index Medicus; Music Index.*

Some specialized periodical indexes of value in historical research are:

*Women's Magazines, 1693–1968.* London: Michael Joseph, 1970. Cynthia White, comp.

*From Radical Left to Extreme Right.* Ann Arbor, Mich.: Campus Publishers, 1970–present. Robert H. Muller et al. This index covers periodicals of dissent and protest.

*\*American Historical Review: General Index for Volumes XLI–LX, 1935–1955.* New York: Macmillan, 1962.

*\*Guide to the American Historical Review, 1895–1945.* Washington, D.C.: Government Printing Office, 1945. Franklin D. Scott and Elaine Tegler, comps. (This work is to be found in American Historical Association, *Annual Report for the Year 1944,* Vol. I, pt. 2, pp. 65–292.)

*Foreign Affairs 50-Year Index: Vols. 1–50, 1922–1972.* New York: Council on Foreign Relations, 1973. Robert J. Palmer, comp.

*The Pacific Historical Review: A Cumulative Index to Volumes I–XLIII, 1932–1974.* Berkeley: University of California Press, 1976. Anne M. Hager and Everett Gordon, comps.

*Fifty Year Index: Mississippi Valley Historical Review, 1914–1964.* Bloomington, Ind.: Organization of American Historians, 1973. Francis J. Krauskopf, comp.

*Index to Economic Journals.* American Economic Association, 1886–present. Homewood, Ill.: R. D. Irwin.

## 5. HISTORICAL PERIODICALS

This is a brief list of some of the best-known historical periodicals. These journals specialize in articles on historical subjects and are written for professional and student researchers. Some have their own cumulative indexes (like that to the *American Historical Review* listed above) and thus can be useful places to begin the search for historical material. There are also many specialized periodicals in history. Be sure to look into those that deal with your topic area.

*Journal of Asian Studies*
*Middle East Journal*
*Slavic Review*
*Journal of Economic History*
*English Historical Review*
*American Historical Review*

*Current History*
*Journal of American History*
*Journal of Southern History*
*Canadian Historical Review*
*Hispanic American Historical Review*
*Journal of Modern History*
*Past and Present*

## 6. GOVERNMENT PUBLICATIONS AND PUBLIC DOCUMENTS

These works are guides to books, pamphlets, speeches, treaties, hearings, reports, etc., published by public agencies. This list, like all others in this appendix, is confined to works in English and is by no means complete. If your research topic is related to governmental affairs at any level, these works can lead you to documents and publications by or about the agencies you are studying. The major publications of the U.S. government are available at many libraries.

### A. INTERNATIONAL AGENCIES

*Guide to League of Nations Publications: A Bibliographical Survey of the Work of the League, 1920–1947.* New York: Columbia University Press, 1951. Hans Aufricht, comp.

*United Nations Documents Index.* New York: United Nations Library, 1950–present. This volume is issued annually.

### B. FOREIGN GOVERNMENT PUBLICATIONS

*Manual of Government Publications, United States and Foreign.* New York: Appleton-Century-Crofts, 1950. Everette S. Brown, comp.

*Great Britain, Parliament: Parliamentary Debates.* London: 1803–present.

## C. UNITED STATES GOVERNMENT PUBLICATIONS

*\*A Popular Guide to Government Publications.* New York: Columbia University Press, 1974. William P. Leidy, comp.

*\*Subject Guide to Major United States Government Publications.* Chicago: American Library Association, 1968. Ellen P. Jackson, comp.

*Monthly Catalogue of United States Government Publications.* Washington, D.C.: Government Printing Office, 1895–present.

*Checklist of United States Public Documents, 1789–1909.* Washington, D.C.: Government Printing Office, 1911, and J. W. Edwards, 1958.

*Catalogue of Public Documents of the United States, 1893–1940.* Washington, D.C.: Government Printing Office, 1895–1945.

*Government Publications and Their Use.* Washington, D.C.: Brookings Institution, 1969. Laurence Schmeckebier and Roy Eastin, eds.

*Subject Guide to Government Reference Books.* Littleton, Colo.: Libraries Unlimited, 1972. Sally Wynkoop, ed.

*Government Publications: A Guide to Bibliographic Tools.* Washington, D.C.: Library of Congress, 1975. Vladimir M. Palic, comp.

*Annotated Bibliography of Bibliographies on Selected Government Publications and Supplementary Guides to the Superintendent of Documents Classification System.* Kalamazoo, Mich.: Western Michigan University, 1967–present. Alexander C. Brody, ed.

*Cumulative Subject Guide to United States Government Bibliographies, 1924–1973.* Arlington, Va.: Carrollton Press, 1976. Edna A. Karely, comp.

*United States Government Publications Relating to the Social Sciences: A Selected, Annotated Guide.* Beverly Hills, Cal.: Sage Publications, 1975. Joseph K. Lu, ed. Chapter II deals with history.

D. UNITED STATES STATE AND LOCAL GOVERNMENT PUBLICATIONS

*State Publications: A Provisional List of Official Publications of the Several States of the United States.* New York: Publishers Weekly, 1908. Richard R. Bowker.

*Bibliography of County Histories of the 3,111 Counties in the United States.* Baltimore: Clarence Peterson, 1946.

For the publications of the state historical societies, see the list of these societies in Appendix B.

## 7. SUBJECT BIBLIOGRAPHIES

A subject bibliography lists printed works on a particular topic. The ones listed here have been chosen with a preference for those that the beginning student is likely to be able to obtain. In this regard, emphasis has been placed on bibliographies that are written especially for students, are of recent publication or republication and therefore likely to have entered new library collections, contain predominantly or solely works in the English language, and are general rather than specialized. Those that are especially useful to beginning students have been designated by an asterisk (*).[2]

A. DISCIPLINES OTHER THAN HISTORY

These bibliographies list works in fields other than history. If an important aspect of your research topic falls under other major branches of knowledge, then valuable materials may exist in nonhistorical publications.

*A Select Bibliography: Asia, Africa, Eastern Europe, Latin America.* New York: American University, 1960, plus supplements. These are studies in the social sciences covering the developing countries of the world.

---

[2]If the title of a bibliography indicates that it is annotated, this means that it not only *lists* books on a particular topic but also provides a brief description of their contents.

For more recent works see *Cumulative Supplement, 1961–1971.*

*Sources of Information in the Social Sciences.* Chicago: American Library Association, 1973. Carl M. White, ed.

*The Humanities: A Selected Guide to Information Sources.* Littleton, Colo.: Libraries Unlimited, 1974. A. Robert Rogers, ed.

*Social Science Research Handbook.* New York: Barnes & Noble, 1974. Raymond G. McInnis and James W. Scott.

B. SPECIALIZED BRANCHES OF HISTORY

*Dictionary of the History of Ideas.* New York: Scribners, 1968–1974. Philip P. Wiener, ed.

*Handbook in the History of Philosophy.* New York: Barnes & Noble, 1961.

*Bibliography on Oral History.* New York: Oral History Association, 1975. Manfred J. Waserman, comp.

*A Bibliography of Psychohistory.* New York: Garland Publishing, 1975. Lloyd deMause, ed.

*Bibliography of the History of Technology.* Cambridge, Mass.: M.I.T. Press, 1968. Eugene S. Ferguson, ed.

*History of Science and Technology: A Select Bibliography for Students.* London: Library Association, 1970. K. J. Rider, ed.

*The New Standard Jewish Encyclopedia.* Garden City, N.Y.: Doubleday, 1977. Geoffrey Wigoder, ed.

C. GENERAL WORLD HISTORY

The remainder of this appendix contains the basic source material for historical research—history bibliographies. Once you have chosen your research topic, these bibliographies and the reference catalog of your library should be your initial step in finding sources on that topic. For convenience to the beginning student, the list of subject bibliographies is separated according to the chronological period or geographical area that the works cover. The bibliographies themselves break down the topics even further.

Don't expect to find an entire bibliography dedicated to

your particular subject. Choose the ones that cover the period or area into which your own topic falls. Remember, your library will probably not have all of these books. If the most promising bibliography is not there, try a different work.

*American Historical Association: A Guide to Historical Literature.* New York: Macmillan, 1961. George F. Howe et al., eds. This work has chapters on all periods and areas, and on many specialized topics.

*Historical Abstracts.* Santa Barbara, Cal.: ABC-Clio, 1955–present. Part A: A Modern History (1450–1914); Part B: The Twentieth Century (1914–present). Eric H. Boehm, ed. This is the best source for articles in history journals.

*A Select Bibliography of History.* Cambridge, Mass.: Henry Adams Club, Dept. of History, Harvard University, 1970. D. David Grose, ed. This work has chapters on all regions and periods.

*Pamphlets.* Washington, D.C.: American Historical Association, Service Center for Teachers, 1956–present. These pamphlets contain narrative and critical essays on a wide range of topics. Each has a bibliography.

*Books for College Libraries.* Chicago: American Library Association, 1975. Melvin Voigt and Joseph Treyz, comps. See Volume III: History. It contains chapters on each geographical area.

*World Historical Fiction Guide.* Metuchen, N.J.: Scarecrow Press, 1973. Daniel McGarry and Sarah White, eds. If you are studying historical novels, this is an important source.

*Books on World History: A Guide for Teachers and Students.* Bloomington: University of Indiana Press, 1973. Warren Wagar, ed.

*A Reader's Guide to Contemporary History.* Chicago: Quadrangle Books, 1972. Bernard Krikler and Walter Laqueur, eds.

D. ANCIENT HISTORY

*Introduction to Ancient History.* Berkeley: University of California, 1970. Herman Bengtson.

*Oxford Classical Dictionary.* Oxford: Clarendon Press, 1970. N. G. L. Hammond and H. H. Scullard, eds.

*International Guide to Classical Studies.* Darien, Conn.: American Bibliographic Service, 1958–present. Annual.

*The Cambridge Ancient History.* Cambridge: Cambridge University Press, 1923–1939, 1951–1954, 1970–1976. This is a multivolume historical work with extensive bibliographies.

*Illustrated Encyclopedia of the Classical World.* New York: Harper & Row, 1975. Michael Avi Yonah and Israel Shatzman, eds.

E. MEDIEVAL HISTORY

\*A *Guide to the Study of Medieval History.* New York: F. S. Crofts & Sons, 1931. Louis J. Paetow. This guide is updated in a supplement by Gray C. Boyce, Medieval Academy of America, 1962.

*International Guide to Medieval Studies.* Darien, Conn.: American Bibliographic Service, 1958–present. Annual.

*Reference Studies in Medieval History.* Chicago: University of Chicago Press, 1925–1930. James W. Thompson.

*History of the Byzantine Empire, 324–1453.* Madison: University of Wisconsin Press, 1952. Alexander Vasiliev. Listed here because of its good bibliography.

*Medieval European History, 395–1500: A Select Bibliography.* London: Historical Association of London, 1963.

*Cambridge Medieval History.* Cambridge: Cambridge University Press, 1911–1936.

*Who's Who in the Middle Ages.* New York: Stein and Day, 1970. John Fines, ed.

F. EARLY MODERN AND MODERN EUROPEAN HISTORY

\**Modern European History, 1494–1789: A Select Bibliography.* London: Historical Association of London, 1966. Alun Davies, comp.

\**Modern European History, 1789–1945: A Select Bibliography.* London: Historical Association of London, 1960. William N. Medlicott, comp.

\**Cambridge Modern History.* Cambridge: Cambridge Uni-

versity Press, 1902–1911; reissued, 1970. These history
volumes have large bibliographies. *The New Cambridge Modern History,* however, has no bibliography.
*A Bibliography of Modern History.* Cambridge: Cambridge University Press, 1968. John Roach, ed. This
bibliography was created to accompany *The New
Cambridge Modern History.*
*Modern European Imperialism: A Bibliography of Books
and Articles, 1815–1972.* Boston: G. K. Hall, 1974.
John P. Halstead, comp.
*Select List of Works on Europe and Europe Overseas,
1715–1815.* Oxford: Clarendon Press, 1956. John
Bromley and A. Goodwin, eds.

G. BRITISH HISTORY

## 1. British History to 1789

*A Bibliography of English History to 1485.* Oxford: Cla-
rendon Press, 1975. Edgar B. Graves, ed.
*Tudor England, 1485–1603: A Bibliographical Handbook.*
Cambridge: Cambridge University Press, 1968. Mor-
timer Levine, comp.
*A Bibliography of British History, 1603–1714.* Oxford:
Clarendon Press, 1970. Mary Keeler, ed.
*Early Modern British History, 1485–1760.* London: His-
torical Association of London, 1970. Helen Miller and
Aubrey Newman, comps.
*A Bibliography of British History, 1714–1789.* Oxford:
Clarendon Press, 1951. Stanley Pargellis and D J Med
ley, eds.

## 2. British History Since 1789

*British History Since 1760: A Select Bibliography.* Lon-
don: Historical Association of London, 1970. Ian R.
Christie, comp.
*A Bibliography of British History, 1789–1851.* Oxford:
Clarendon Press, 1977. Lucy Brown and Ian R.
Christie, eds.
*Victorian England, 1837–1901: A Bibliographic Hand-
book.* Cambridge: Cambridge University Press, 1970.
J. Altholz, comp.

*A Bibliography of British History, 1851–1914.* Oxford: Clarendon Press, 1976. H. J. Hanham, ed.

*Modern England, 1901–1970: A Bibliographical Handbook.* Cambridge: Cambridge University Press, 1976. Alfred F. Havighurst, comp.

3. *Irish, Scottish, and British Empire History*

*Irish History: A Select Bibliography.* London: Historical Association of London, 1969. Edith M. Johnson, comp.

*A Bibliography of Works Related to Scotland, 1916–1950.* Edinburgh: Edinburgh University Press, 1959–1960. P. D. Hancock, ed.

*Cambridge History of the British Empire.* Cambridge: Cambridge University Press, 1929–1959. John Rose, Arthur Newton, and Ernest Benians, comps.

H. EAST EUROPEAN HISTORY

*\*The Soviet Union and Eastern Europe.* New York: Praeger, 1970. George Schoepflin. This is a general handbook but includes bibliographies.

*The American Bibliography of Slavic and East European Studies.* Columbus, Ohio: American Association for the Advancement of Slavic Studies, 1957–present.

*Junior Slavica: A Selected, Annotated Bibliography of Books in English on Russia and Eastern Europe.* Littleton, Colo.: Libraries Unlimited, 1968. Stephan M. Horak, ed.

*\*The Balkans Since 1453.* New York: Rinehart, 1958. Leften S. Stavrianos. There is an extensive bibliography at the end of this work.

*Bibliography of American Publications on East Central Europe 1945–1957.* Bloomington: Indiana University Press, 1958. Robert F. Byrnes, ed.

I. RUSSIAN HISTORY (AND USSR)

*Junior Slavica: A Selected, Annotated Bibliography of Books in English on Russia and Eastern Europe.* Littleton, Colo.: Libraries Unlimited, 1968. Stephan M. Horak, ed.

*The Soviet Union and Eastern Europe.* New York: Praeger, 1970. George Schoepflin.

*The American Bibliography of Slavic and East European Studies.* Columbus, Ohio: American Association for the Advancement of Slavic Studies, 1957–present.

*\*A Bibliography of Works in English on Early Russian History to 1800.* New York: Barnes & Noble, 1969. Peter A. Crowther, comp.

*\*Books in English on the Soviet Union, 1917–1973: A Bibliography.* New York: Garland Publishing, 1975. David L. Jones, comp.

*\*A Select Bibliography of Works in English on Russian History, 1801–1917.* Oxford: Blackwell, 1962. David Shapiro, ed.

*\*Encyclopedia of Russia and the Soviet Union.* New York: McGraw-Hill, 1961. Michael T. Florinsky, ed.

*\*A History of Soviet Russia.* London: Macmillan, 1950–1960. Edward H. Carr. See bibliography at end of work.

*An Atlas of Russian History.* New Haven, Conn.: Yale University Press, 1970. Allen F. Chew, ed.

J. AFRICAN HISTORY[3]

*Cambridge History of Africa.* Cambridge: Cambridge University Press, 1975–present.

*Africa South of the Sahara: A Bibliography for Undergraduate Libraries.* Williamsport, Pa.: Bro-Dart, 1971. Peter Duignan, ed.

*Africa and the West: An Introduction to the History of Sub-Saharan Africa from Antiquity to 1840.* San Francisco: Chandler, 1972. Peter Duignan and Lewis H. Gann, eds.

*The African Experience.* Evanston, Ill.: Northwestern University Press, 1970. John N. Paden and Edward W. Soja, eds.

*History of Africa in Maps.* Chicago: Denoyer-Geppert, 1967. Harry A. Gailey.

*Historical Dictionary of* ———. Metuchen, N.J.: Scarecrow Press, 1972–1976. This is a series of historical dictionaries including separate volumes for most African nations.

[3]For the northern African states that border on the Mediterranean, see Near and Middle Eastern History.

*African Newspapers in Selected American Libraries.* Washington, D.C.: Library of Congress, 1962.

*\*A Select Bibliography on Traditional and Modern Africa.* Syracuse, N.Y.: Syracuse University Press, 1968. Peter Gutkind and John B. Webster, eds.

*African Affairs for the General Reader: A Selected and Introductory Bibliographic Guide.* New York: Council of the African-American Institute, 1967. African Bibliographic Center.

*Current Themes in African Historical Studies: A Selected Bibliographical Guide to Resources for Research in African History.* Westport, Conn.: Negro Universities Press, 1970. Daniel G. Matthews, ed.

K. NEAR AND MIDDLE EASTERN HISTORY

*\*The Near and Middle East: An Introduction to History and Bibliography.* Washington, D.C.: American Historical Association, 1959. Roderic H. Davidson, ed.

*Concise Encyclopedia of the Middle East.* Washington, D.C.: Public Affairs Press, 1973. Mehdi Heravi, ed.

*The Arabian Peninsula: A Selected, Annotated List of Periodicals, Books and Articles in English.* Washington, D.C.: Library of Congress, 1951.

*\*The Islamic Near East and North Africa: An Annotated Guide to Books in English for Non-Specialists.* Littleton, Colo.: Libraries Unlimited, 1977. David W. Littlefield, ed.

*Middle East and Islam: A Bibliographical Introduction.* Geneva: Inter Documentation, 1972. Derek Hopwood and Diana Grimwood-Jones, eds.

*Middle East and North Africa: A Bibliography for Undergraduate Libraries.* Williamsport, Pa.: Bro-Dart, 1971. Harry N. Howard, ed.

*The Arab-Israeli Conflict: A Historical, Political, Social and Military Bibliography.* Santa Barbara, Cal.: ABC-Clio, 1976. Ronald M. Devore, ed.

*\*Concise Encyclopedia of Arabic Civilizations.* New York: Praeger, 1960–1966. Stephan and Nandy Ronart, eds.

*Atlas of Islamic History.* Princeton, N.J.: Princeton University Press, 1954. Harry W. Hazard, ed.

*Books on Asia from the Near East to the Far East: A
Guide for General Readers.* Toronto: University of
Toronto Press, 1971. Eleazir Birnbaum, ed.

## L. GENERAL ASIAN HISTORY

*Cumulative Bibliography of Asian Studies, 1941–1965.*
Boston: G. K. Hall, 1970.

*East Asia: A Bibliography for Undergraduate Libraries.*
Williamsport, Pa.: Bro-Dart, 1970. Donald G. Gillian
et al., eds. This book is written for librarians but can
be used by students as well.

*Outline Atlas of Eastern History.* London: Edward Arnold, 1954. Roger R. Sellman, ed.

*Books on Asia from the Near East to the Far East: A
Guide for General Readers.* Toronto: University of
Toronto Press, 1971. Eleazir Birnbaum, ed.

*Oriental and Asian Bibliography.* Hamden, Conn.: Ar-
chon, 1966. J. D. Pearson, ed.

*Asia: A Selected and Annotated Guide to Reference
Works.* Cambridge, Mass.: M.I.T. Press, 1971. G. Raymond Nunn, ed.

*Bibliography of Asian Studies.* Ann Arbor, Mich.: Association for Asian Studies, 1941–present.

*Historical and Cultural Dictionary of* ————. Metuchen, N.J.: Scarecrow Press, 1972–present. This is a
series of dictionaries including separate volumes for
most Asian nations.

### 1. Indian, Pakistani, and Ceylonese History

*India: A Critical Bibliography.* Tucson: University of
Arizona Press, 1964. J. Michael Mahar, ed.

*A Dictionary of Indian History.* New York: Braziller, 1967.
Sachchidananda Bhattacharya.

*The History of India: Its Study and Interpretation.* Washington, D.C.: American Historical Association, 1958.
Robert D. Crane.

*Introduction to the Civilization of India: Handbook.* Chicago: University of Chicago Press, 1961.

*Cambridge History of India.* New York: Macmillan,
1922–1937. See bibliography at end of volumes.

*An Historical Atlas of the Indian Peninsula.* New York: Oxford University Press, 1959. Cuthbert C. Davies, ed.

*South Asia: A Selected Bibliography on India, Pakistan and Ceylon.* New York: American Institute of Pacific Relations, 1957. Patrick Wilson, ed.

*South Asia: An Introductory Bibliography.* Chicago: University of Chicago Press, 1962. Maureen Patterson and R. B. Inden, eds.

2. *Southeast Asian History*

*\*Southeast Asia: A Critical Bibliography.* Tucson: University of Arizona Press, 1969. Kennedy G. Tregonning, ed.

*\*Southeast Asian History: A Bibliographic Guide.* New York: Praeger, 1962. Stephen Hay and Margaret Case, eds.

*A Guide to Books on Southeast Asian History* [1961–1966]. Santa Barbara, Cal.: ABC-Clio, 1969. Gayle Morrison, comp.

*Southeast Asia: An Annotated Bibliography.* Westport, Conn.: Greenwood Press, 1968. Cecil C. Hobbs, ed.

*Vietnam: A Comprehensive Bibliography.* Metuchen, N.J.: Scarecrow Press, 1973. John H. M. Chen, ed.

*The Vietnam Conflict.* Santa Barbara, Cal.: ABC-Clio, 1973. Milton Leitenberg and Richard D. Burns, comps.

*A Bibliography on the Political and Administrative History of Vietnam, 1802–1962.* East Lansing: Michigan State University; Vietnam Advisory Group, 1962. Roy Jumper, ed.

3. *Chinese History*

*\*China: A Critical Bibliography.* Tucson: University of Arizona Press, 1962. Charles O. Hucker, ed.

*\*Chinese History: A Bibliographical Review.* Washington, D.C.: American Historical Association, 1958. Charles O. Hucker, ed.

*Historical Atlas of China.* Chicago: Aldine, 1966. Albert Herrmann, ed.

*China and America: A Bibliography of Interactions, For-*

*eign and Domestic.* Honolulu: University of Hawaii Press, 1972. James M. McCutcheon, comp.

### 4. Japanese and Korean History

*\*Japanese History: New Dimensions of Approach and Understanding.* Washington, D.C.: American Historical Association, 1961. John W. Hall, ed.

*\*Japan and Korea: A Critical Bibliography.* Tucson: University of Arizona Press, 1962. Bernard Silberman, ed.

*A Guide to Reference and Research Materials on Korean History: An Annotated Bibliography.* Honolulu: East-West Center, 1968. William E. Hentworth, ed.

*Dictionary of Japanese History.* New York: Walker, 1968. Joseph M. Goedertier.

### M. LATIN AMERICAN AND CARIBBEAN HISTORY

*Handbook of Latin American Studies.* Cambridge, Mass.: Harvard University Press, 1936–1947 and Gainesville: University of Florida Press, 1948–present. Annual volume.

*\*Latin America: A Guide to the Historical Literature.* Austin: University of Texas Press, 1971. Charles C. Griffin, ed.

*A Guide to Latin American Studies.* Los Angeles: University of California, 1967. Martin H. Sable, ed.

*\*Latin American History: A Guide to the Literature in English.* New York: Oxford University Press, 1958. R. A. Humphreys, ed. ⟨

*Latin America and the Caribbean: A Bibliographic Guide to Works in English.* Coral Gables: University of Miami Press, 1967. Stojan A. Bayitch, ed.

*\*Latin America and the Caribbean: A Handbook.* New York: Praeger, 1968. Claudio Veliz, ed.

*Who's Who in Latin America.* Stanford: Stanford University Press, 1951. Reprinted by Blaine Ethridge Books, Detroit, 1971. Ronald Hilton, ed.

*\*Guide to the Hispanic American Historical Review, 1945–1955.* Durham, N.C.: Duke University Press, 1958. Charles Gibson, ed. The years 1918 to 1945 are indexed by Ruth L. Butler.

*Index to Latin American Periodical Literature, 1929–1960.* New York: G. K. Hall, 1962. Pan American Union.

*\*Latin America, Spain and Portugal: A Selected and Annotated Bibliographical Guide to Books Published in the United States, 1954–1974.* Metuchen, N.J.: Scarecrow Press, 1977. A. C. Wilgus, ed. and comp.

*Latin America: A Guide to Economic History, 1830–1930.* Berkeley: University of California Press, 1977. Stanley Stein and R. Cortés Conde, eds.

*Encyclopedia of Latin America.* New York: McGraw-Hill, 1974. Helen Delpar, ed.

*Historical Dictionary of* ————. Metuchen, N.J.: Scarecrow Press. This is a series of historical dictionaries including separate volumes for most Latin American nations.

N. CANADIAN HISTORY

*Encyclopedia Canadiana.* Toronto: Grolier, 1972.

*Bibliographia Canadiana.* Don Mills, Ont.: Longman Canada Limited, 1973. Claude Thibault, comp.

*The Oxford Companion to Canadian History and Literature.* Toronto: Oxford University Press, 1967, 1973. Norah Story, comp.

*Dictionary of Canadian Biography.* Toronto: University of Toronto Press, 1966–present.

O. UNITED STATES HISTORY

In the case of United States history, the bibliographies have been broken down in terms of certain topics of special interest to students.

Many of this first group of bibliographies have separate chapters on specialized topics.

*\*Harvard Guide to American History.* Cambridge, Mass.: Harvard University Press, 1974. Oscar Handlin et al., eds. Chapters six through thirty contain detailed reading lists for many periods and topics in United States history. References are to books and articles written prior to 1971.

*Writings on American History.* Washington, D.C.: American Historical Association, 1956 and Millwood, N.Y.: KTO Press, 1976. The original series of volumes covers (with two brief lapses) books and articles written between 1902 and 1959. The new series is now annual and covers only articles written since 1960.

*America: History and Life.* Santa Barbara, Cal.: ABC-Clio Press, 1954–present. Each volume now has three parts: (A) annotations of journal articles, (B) index to book reviews, and (C) a bibliography of books, articles, and dissertations.

*American Historical Association: A Guide to Historical Literature.* New York: Macmillan, 1961. See chapter on United States history.

*A Bibliography of American Autobiographies.* Madison: University of Wisconsin Press, 1961. Louis Kaplan et al., comps. An important source if you are researching the life of a historical figure.

*Dictionary of American History.* New York: Scribners, 1942–1961. James T. Adams and Roy V. Coleman, eds. Revised, 1976

*Concise Dictionary of American History.* New York: Scribners, 1962. Thomas C. Cochran and Wayne Andrews, eds.

*U.S.-iana, 1650–1950: A Selective Bibliography.* New York: Bowker, 1962. Wright Howes, ed.

*American Social History Since 1860.* Northbrook, Ill.: AHM Publishing, 1970. Robert H. Bremner, comp.

*American Social History Before 1860.* Northbrook, Ill.: AHM Publishing, 1970. Gerald N. Grob, comp.

*Encyclopedia of American History.* New York: Harper & Row, 1976. Richard B. Morris, ed.

*The American Heritage Pictorial Atlas of United States History.* New York: American Heritage Publishing Co., 1966.

*A Guide to the Study of the United States of America.* Washington, D.C.: Library of Congress, 1960. Supplement, 1976. This work covers all fields of knowledge. It has several chapters on aspects of United States history.

For sources on the United States government, see "United States Government Publications" on pages 120–121.

## 1. Regional, State, County, and Local United States History

The sources listed here can be supplemented by the appropriate sections of the *Harvard Guide to American History*, *Writings on American History*, and *America: History and Life*.

*A Classified Bibliography of the Periodical Literature of the Trans-Mississippi West, 1811–1967*. Bloomington: Indiana University Press, 1961, 1970. Oscar O. Winther, ed.

*Directory of State and Local History Periodicals*. Chicago: American Library Association, 1970. Milton Crouch and Hans Raum, comps.

*The Frontier and the American West*. Northbrook, Ill.: AHM Publishing, 1976. Rodman W. Paul and Richard W. Etulain, comps.

*The Old South*. Northbrook, Ill.: AHM Publishing, forthcoming. Fletcher M. Greene and J. Isaac Copeland, comps.

*The New South*. Northbrook, Ill.: AHM Publishing, forthcoming. Paul M. Gaston, comp.

*Bibliography of County Histories of the 3,111 Counties in the United States*. Baltimore: Clarence Peterson, 1946.

*\*Directory: Historical Societies and Agencies in the United States and Canada, 1975*. Nashville: American Association for State and Local History, 1975. Donna McDonald, ed. This volume includes the addresses of state and local historical societies.

*Consolidated Bibliography of County Histories, 1935–1961*. Baltimore: Genealogical Publishing Co., 1963. Clarence S. Peterson, comp.

*Localized History Series*. New York: Teachers College Press, 1965–present. Clifford L. Lord, ed. A multivolume series; each volume contains a bibliography of works on a separate state, region, city, or ethnic group.

*United States Local Histories in the Library of Congress:*

*A Bibliography.* Baltimore: Magna Carta, 1975. Marion J. Kaminkow, ed.

## 2. Specific Periods

The best bibliographies for the study of specific periods of United States history are the Goldentree Series published by AHM Publishing Corporation, Northbrook, Ill. The relevant items in this series, in chronological order, are listed below.

*The American Colonies in the Seventeenth Century* (1971). Alden T. Vaughan, comp.
*The American Colonies in the Eighteenth Century, 1689–1763* (1969). Jack P. Greene, comp.
*The American Revolution* (1973). John Shy, comp.
*Confederation, Constitution and Early National Period, 1781–1815* (1975). E. James Ferguson, comp.
*American Nationalism and Sectionalism, 1816–1841* (forthcoming). Edwin A. Miles and Robert Remini, comps.
*Manifest Destiny and the Coming of the Civil War, 1841–1860* (1970). Don E. Fehrenbacher, comp.
*The Nation in Crisis, 1861–1877* (1969). David Donald, comp.
*The Gilded Age, 1877–1896* (1973). Vincent P. DeSantis, comp.
*The Progressive Era and the Great War, 1896–1920* (1969). Arthur S. Link and W. M. Leary, Jr., comps.
*The Twenties and the New Deal, 1920–1940* (forthcoming). Robert E. Burke and Richard Lowitt, comps.
*The Second World War and the Atomic Age, 1940–1973* (1975). E. David Cronon and Theodore B. Rosenof.

## 3. Diplomatic History

*Guide to the Diplomatic History of the United States, 1775–1921.* Washington, D.C.: Government Printing Office, 1935. Samuel F. Bemis and Grace G. Griffin, eds.
*Index to United States Documents Relating to Foreign Affairs, 1828–1861.* Washington, D.C.: Carnegie Institute, 1914–1921. Adelaide R. Hasse, ed.

*Treaties and Other International Acts of the United States of America*. Washington, D.C.: Government Printing Office, 1931–present. D. Hunter Miller, ed.

*\*Foreign Affairs Bibliography: A Selected and Annotated List of Books on International Relations* [1919–present]. New York: Harper & Row, 1933, 1943, 1953 and R. R. Bowker, 1964. Vol. I covers 1919–1932; Vol. II, 1932–1942; Vol. III, 1942–1952; Vol. IV, 1952–1962; Vol. V, 1962–1972.

*\*Foreign Relations of the United States*. Washington, D.C.: Government Printing Office, 1861–present. United States Department of State. These volumes are issued annually and contain actual diplomatic correspondence. These are *primary* sources rather than bibliographies. They are listed because most libraries have them.

*General Index to the Published Volumes of the Diplomatic Correspondence of the United States, 1861–1899*. Washington, D.C.: Government Printing Office, 1902. United States Department of State.

*A Bibliography of United States–Latin American Relations Since 1810*. Lincoln: University of Nebraska Press, 1968. David F. Trask et al, eds.

*American Diplomatic History Before 1900*. Northbrook, Ill.: AHM Publishing, 1978. Norman A. Graebner.

*American Diplomatic History Since 1890*. Northbrook, Ill.: AHM Publishing, 1975. Winton B. Fowler, comp.

4. *Labor History*

*Labor History in the United States: A General Bibliography*. Urbana: University of Illinois, Institute of Labor and Industrial Relations, 1962. Gene S. Stroud and Gilbert E. Donahue, eds.

*American Labor History in Journals of History: A Bibliography*. Urbana: University of Illinois, Institute of Labor and Industrial Relations, 1962. Fred D. Rose, ed.

*Labor Unions*. Westport, Conn.: Greenwood Press, 1977. Gary M. Fink, ed. Contains a brief history and bibliography for each major union.

*American Labor History and Comparative Labor Move-*

*ments.* Tucson: University of Arizona Press, 1973. James C. McBrearty, comp.

## 5. Business and Economic History

*The Economic History of the United States Prior to 1860: An Annotated Bibliography.* Santa Barbara, Cal.: ABC-Clio, 1976. Thomas Orsagh et al., eds.

*\*American Economic History Before 1860.* Northport, Ill.: AHM Publishing, 1969. George R. Taylor, comp.

*\*American Economic History Since 1860.* Northport, Ill.: AHM Publishing, 1971. Edward C. Kirkland, comp.

*American Economic and Business History: A Guide to Information Sources.* Detroit: Gale Research, 1971. Robert W. Lovett, ed.

*Guide to Business History.* Cambridge, Mass.: Harvard University Press, 1948. Henrietta M. Larson, ed.

## 6. Black History

*A Bibliography of Antislavery in America.* Ann Arbor: University of Michigan Press, 1961. Dwight L. Dumond, ed.

*\*A Layman's Guide to Negro History.* New York: McGraw-Hill, 1967. Erwin A. Salk, ed.

*\*The Negro in America: A Bibliography.* Cambridge, Mass.: Harvard University Press, 1970. Elizabeth W. Miller, comp.

*\*A Bibliographic History of Blacks in America Since 1528.* New York: McKay, 1971. Edgar A. Toppin, ed.

*The Negro in the United States: A Research Guide.* Bloomington: University of Indiana Press, 1965. Erwin K. Welsch, ed.

*\*Blacks in America: Bibliographical Essays.* Garden City, N.Y.: Doubleday, 1971. James M. McPherson et al.

*Black History Viewpoints: A Selected Bibliographical Guide to Resources for Afro-American and African History.* Westport, Conn.: African Bibliographic Center, 1969.

*Black Studies: A Bibliography for the Use of Schools, Libraries and the General Reader.* Brooklawn, N.J.: McKinley, 1973. Leonard B. Irwin, comp.

*The Negro in the United States: A Selected Bibliography.*
Washington, D.C.: Library of Congress, 1970, and
University Microfilms, 1969. Dorothy B. Porter, ed.
*Afro-American History: A Bibliography.* Millwood, N.Y.:
KTO Press, 1972. Dwight L. Smith, ed.
*The Black American Reference Book.* Englewood Cliffs,
N.J.: Prentice-Hall, 1976. Mabel M. Smythe, ed.

7. *Mexican-American History*

*Mexican-American History: A Critical Selective Bibliogra-
phy.* Santa Barbara, Cal.: Mexican-American Historical
Society, 1969.
*The Mexican American: A Selected and Annotated Bibli-
ography.* Stanford, Cal.: Stanford University Press,
1971. Luis G. Nogales, ed.
*Bibliografía de Aztlán: An Annotated Chicano Bibliogra-
phy.* San Diego, Cal.: San Diego State College, 1971.
Ernie Barrios, comp.
*The Mexican American: A Selected and Annotated Bibli-
ography.* Stanford, Cal.: Stanford University Press,
1969. John J. Johnson, ed.
*A Bibliography for Chicano History.* San Francisco: R &
E Research Associates, 1972. Matt S. Meier and Feli-
ciano Rivera, comps.
*Reference Materials on Mexican Americans: An Annotated
Bibliography.* Metuchen, N.J.: Scarecrow Press, 1976.
Richard P. Woods, ed.

8. *Puerto Rican History*

*Puerto Ricans on the United States Mainland.* Totowa,
N.J.: Rowman and Littlefield, 1972. Francesco Cor-
dasco, ed.
*The Puerto Ricans: An Annotated Bibliography.* New
York: Bowker, 1973. Paquita Vivó, ed.
*An Annotated, Selected Puerto Rican Bibliography.* New
York: Columbia University Press, 1972. Enrique R.
Bravo, comp.
*The Puerto Ricans 1493–1973: A Chronology and Fact
Book.* Dobbs Ferry, N.Y.: Oceana, 1973. Francesco
Cordasco, ed.

*Bibliography of Puerto Ricans in the United States.* New York: Department of Labor, Commonwealth of Puerto Rico, 1959. Clarence Senior, ed

*The Spanish Speaking in the United States: A Guide to Materials.* Washington, D.C.: Cabinet Commission on Opportunities for the Spanish Speaking, 1971.

*Historical Dictionary of Puerto Rico and the Virgin Islands.* Metuchen, N.J.: Scarecrow Press, 1973. Kenneth Farr, comp.

## 9. Women's History

*The American Woman in Colonial and Revolutionary Times, 1565–1800: A Syllabus with Bibliography.* Philadelphia: University of Pennsylvania Press, 1962. Eurenie Leonard et al.

*Women's Magazines, 1693–1968.* London: Michael Joseph, 1970. Cynthia White, comp.

*\*Index to Women of the World from Ancient to Modern Times.* Westwood, Mass.: Faxon, 1970. Norma O. Ireland.

*\*Notable American Women, 1607–1950: A Bibliographical Dictionary.* Cambridge, Mass.: Harvard University Press, 1971. Edward T. James, ed.

*Women: A Bibliography on Their Education and Careers.* Washington, D.C.: Human Services Press, 1971. Helen S. Astin et al., eds.

*Women in American History.* Santa Barbara, Cal.: ABC-Clio, 1978. Cynthia E. Harrison, ed.

## 10. General Immigrant and Ethnic History

These are the best bibliographies to use if you are researching the history of a minority group not listed separately in this appendix or if you are unsure which group you wish to study.

*\*Minority Studies: A Select Annotated Bibliography.* Boston: G. K. Hall, 1975. Priscilla Oaks, ed.

*\*A Handbook of American Minorities.* New York: New York University Press, 1976. Wayne C. Miller.

*A Comprehensive Bibliography for the Study of American*

*Minorities.* New York: New York University Press,
1976. Wayne C. Miller.
*Brief Ethnic Bibliography: An Annotated Guide to the
Ethnic Experience in the United States.* Cambridge,
Eng.: Langdon Associates, 1976. Joseph J. Barton,
comp.
*Ethnic and Racial Minorities in America: A Select Bibli-
ography of the Geographical Literature.* Monticello,
Ill.: Council of Planning Librarians, 1973. John A.
Jackle, ed.
*Encyclopedic Dictionary of Ethnic Newspapers and Peri-
odicals in the United States.* Littleton, Colo.: Li-
braries Unlimited, 1972. Lubomyr S. Wynar, ed.

## 11. European Immigrant and Ethnic History

*\*European Immigration and Ethnicity in the United
States and Canada: A Bibliography.* Santa Barbara,
Cal.: ABC-Clio, 1979. David L. Brye, ed.
*Italians in the United States: A Bibliography of Reports,
Texts, Critical Studies and Related Materials.* New
York: Oriole Editions, 1972. Francesco Cordasco and
Salvatore La Gumina, eds.
*Hungarians in America: A Biographical Dictionary.* Phila-
delphia: Alpha Publications, 1971. Desi K. Bognar, ed.
*A Bibliographic Guide to Greeks in the United States,
1890–1968.* New York: Center for Migration Studies,
1970. Michael N. Cutsumbis, ed.
*German-Americana: A Bibliography.* Metuchen, N.J.:
Scarecrow Press, 1975. Don Heinrich Tolzmann,
comp.
*The British in America 1578–1970: A Chronology and
Fact Book.* Dobbs Ferry, N.Y.: Oceana, 1972. Howard
B. Furer, ed. Volume covers the English, Scotch,
Welsh, and Scotch-Irish.
*The ——— in America: A Chronology and Fact Book.*
Dobbs Ferry, N.Y.: Oceana, 1971–present. This is a
series with separate volumes on the Germans, Scandi-
navians, Italians, Poles, Dutch, Jews, Hungarians, and
others.

## 12. Asian Immigrant and Ethnic History

*Asian Americans: An Annotated Bibliography for Public Libraries.* Chicago: American Library Association, 1977.

*Asians in America: A Selected, Annotated Bibliography.* Davis: University of California, Department of Applied Behavioral Sciences, 1971. Isao Fujimoto, ed.

*China and America: A Bibliography of Interactions, Foreign and Domestic.* Honolulu: University of Hawaii Press, 1972. James M. McCutcheon, comp.

## 13. American Indian History

*Handbook of American Indians North of Mexico.* New York: Pageant, 1959. Frederick W. Hodge et al. This is a reprint of a 1910 work.

*Reference Encyclopedia of the American Indian.* New York: B. Klein and Company, 1967, and Rye, N.Y.: Todd, 1973. Bernard Klein and Daniel Icolari, eds.

*Index to Literature on the American Indian.* n.p.: Indian Historian Press, 1972. American Indian Historical Society.

*The American Indian 1492–1970: A Chronology and Fact Book.* Dobbs Ferry, N.Y.: Oceana, 1971. Henry C. Dennis, ed.

*\*Indians of the United States and Canada: A Bibliography.* Millwood, N.Y.: KTO Press, 1974. Dwight L. Smith, ed.

*Ethnographic Bibliography of North America.* New Haven, Conn.: HRAF Press, 1975. George P. Murdock and Timothy J. O'Leary, eds.

## 14. Miscellaneous Topics

*A Critical Bibliography of Religion in America.* Princeton, N.J.: Princeton University Press, 1961. Nelson R. Burr, ed.

*Religion in American Life.* Northbrook, Ill.: AHM Publishing, 1971. Nelson R. Burr, comp.

*American Constitutional Development.* Northbrook, Ill.: AHM Publishing, 1977. Alpheus T. Mason, comp.

*The History of American Education.* Northbrook, Ill.:
AHM Publishing, 1976. Jurgen Herbst, comp.
*American Urban Development.* Northbrook, Ill.: AHM
Publishing, forthcoming. Richard C. Wade, comp.
*Bibliography of North American Folklore and Folksong.*
New York: Dover Publications, 1961. Charles Hay-
wood, ed.
*Era of the American Revolution: A Bibliography.* Santa
Barbara, Cal.: ABC-Clio, 1975. Dwight L. Smith, ed.
*Civil War Books: A Critical Bibliography.* Baton Rouge:
Louisiana State University Press, 1967–1968. Allan
Nevins, ed.
*Bibliographic Guide to the Two World Wars.* New York:
Bowker, 1977. Gwyn M. Bayliss, ed.
*World War II: Books in English, 1945–1965.* Stanford,
Cal.: Hoover Institution, 1971. Janet Ziegler, comp. ₄
*Dictionary of Social Reform.* New York: Philosophical Li-
brary, 1963. Louis Filler.
*Communism in the United States: A Bibliography.* Ithaca,
N.Y.: Cornell University Press, 1969. Joel I. Seidman,
ed. and comp.

## 8. SOURCES FOR HISTORICAL STATISTICS AND OTHER QUANTITATIVE DATA

*Historical Tables, 58 B.C.–A.D. 1955.* New York: St. Mar-
tin's Press, 1956. Sigfrid H. Steinberg.
*Bibliography of Selected Statistical Sources on the Ameri-
can Nations.* Washington, D.C.: Inter-American Statis-
tical Institute, 1947.
*\*Historical Statistics of the United States, Colonial Times
to 1970.* Washington, D.C.: Bureau of the Census,
1976.
*\*Statistical Abstract of the United States.* Washington,
D.C.: Government Printing Office, 1878–present.
Annual.
*Statistical Yearbooks: An Annotated Bibliography of the
General Statistical Yearbooks of Major Political Sub-
divisions of the World.* Washington, D.C.: Library of
Congress, 1953.

*Demographic Yearbook.* New York: United Nations Statistical Office, 1949–present. Annual.

*Population Index.* Princeton, N.J.: Office of Population Research, 1935–present.

*\*European Historical Statistics, 1750–1970.* Berkeley: University of California Press, 1975. B. R. Mitchell, ed.

*Statistical Yearbook.* New York: United Nations Statistical Office, 1949–present.

## 9. GUIDES TO PHOTOCOPIED AND NONPRINTED SOURCES

*American Historical Association Guide to Photocopied Historical Materials in the United States and Canada.* Ithaca, N.Y.: Cornell University Press, 1961. Richard W. Hale, ed.

*Union List of Microfilms.* Ann Arbor, Mich.: J. W. Edwards, 1951. Eleanor E. Campion, comp.

*List of National Archives Microfilm Publications.* Washington, D.C.: National Archives and Records Service, 1961.

*Subject Guide to Microfilms in Print.* Washington, D.C.: Microcard Editions, 1962–present. Albert J. Diaz, ed.

*Guide to the Special Collections of Prints and Photographs in the Library of Congress.* Washington, D.C.: Government Printing Office, 1955. Paul Vanderbilt, ed.

*Library of Congress Catalogue: Motion Pictures and Filmstrips.* Washington, D.C.: Library of Congress, 1953–present. Annual.

*Library of Congress Catalogue: Music and Phonorecords.* Washington, D.C.: Library of Congress, 1953–present. Annual.

*Picture Sources: An Introductory List.* New York: Special Libraries Association, 1959. Helen Faye, ed.

*The Oral History Collection of Columbia University.* New York: Columbia University Oral History Research Office, 1964.

*Oral History in the United States: A Directory.* New York: Oral History Association, 1971. Gary L. Shumway, comp. Locates and describes oral history collections.

## 10.  *GUIDES TO ABSTRACTS, ARCHIVES, DISSERTATIONS, AND CURRENT RESEARCH*

*Dissertation Abstracts: Abstracts of Dissertations and Monographs in Microfilm*. Ann Arbor, Mich.: University Microfilms, 1961.

*A Guide to Archives and Manuscripts in the United States*. New Haven, Conn.: Yale University Press, 1961. Philip C. Hamer, ed.

*The National Union Catalog of Manuscript Collections*. Ann Arbor, Mich.: J. W. Edwards, 1962. Library of Congress Catalogue.

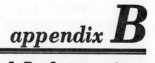

appendix *B*

# Useful Information
# for the Historian

### State Historical Societies

If your topic concerns the history of a particular state, one of the best sources of information is the state historical societies. These groups maintain archives, do research, publish journals, and do other tasks concerning the histories of their states. They can also help you locate information on county and local history. By writing to or visiting these societies you can find out if books or archives on state or local history are located near enough to your school to be useful as part of your research. Access to archival materials can make history research very exciting. Most towns, especially if they are county seats (the town in which county governments are located) keep local and county records, many of which may be available to the public. If your school or home is located in a large city,

*145*

there will likely be one or more private or city historical societies.

If you desire information on state or local history and you are aware of no source close by, contact the appropriate state historical society.

Alabama Historical Association, 3121 Carlisle Road, Birmingham, 35213.

Arizona Historical Society, 949 East 2nd Street, Tucson, 85719.

Arkansas Historical Association, History Department, University of Arkansas, Fayetteville, 71703.

California Historical Society, 2090 Jackson Street, San Francisco, 94115.

State Historical Society of Colorado, 200 Fourteenth Avenue, Denver, 80203.

Connecticut Historical Society, 1 Elizabeth Street, Hartford, 06105.

Historical Society of Delaware, 505 Market Street, Wilmington, 19801.

Florida Historical Society, University of South Florida Library, Tampa, 33620.

Georgia Historical Commission, 116 Mitchell Street, S.W., Atlanta, 30303.

Hawaiian Historical Society, 560 Kawaiahao Street, Honolulu, 96813.

Idaho State Historical Society, 610 N. Julia Davis Drive, Boise, 83706.

Illinois State Historical Society, Old State Capitol Building, Springfield, 62706.

Indiana Historical Bureau, State Library and History Building, Indianapolis, 46204.

Iowa State Department of History and Archives, East 12th Street and Grand Avenue, Des Moines, 50319.

Kansas State Historical Society, Memorial Building, 120 West 10th Street, Topeka, 66612.

Kentucky Historical Society, Box H, Frankfort, 40601.

Louisiana Historical Association, Box 44422, Capitol Station, Baton Rouge, 70804.

Maine Historical Society, 487 Congress Street, Portland, 04111.

Maryland Historical Society, 201 West Monument Street at Park Avenue, Baltimore, 21202.

Massachusetts Historical Society, 1154 Boylston Street, Boston, 02215.

Historical Society of Michigan, 2117 Washtenaw Avenue, Ann Arbor, 48104.

Minnesota Historical Society, 690 Cedar Street, St. Paul, 55101.

Mississippi Historical Society, Box 571, Jackson, 39205.

Missouri Historical Society, Jefferson Memorial Building, St. Louis, 63112.

Montana Historical Society, 225 North Roberts Street, Helena, 59601.

Nebraska State Historical Society, 1500 R Street, Lincoln, 68508.

New Hampshire Historical Society, 30 Park Street, Concord, 03301.

New Jersey Historical Commission, State Library, 185 West State Street, Trenton, 08625.

Historical Society of New Mexico, Box 1442, Socorro, 87801.

New York State Historical Association, Lake Street, Cooperstown, New York, 13326.

North Carolina State Department of Archives and History, 109 East Jones Street, Raleigh, 27602.

State Historical Society of North Dakota, Liberty Memorial Building, Bismarck, 58501.

Ohio Historical Society, Ohio Historical Center, Columbus, 43211.

Oklahoma Historical Society, Historical Building, Oklahoma City, 73105.

Oregon Historical Society, 1230 S.W. Park Avenue, Portland, 97205.

Pennsylvania Historical and Museum Commission, Box 1026, Harrisburg, 17108.

Rhode Island Historical Society, 52 Power Street, Providence, 02906.

South Carolina Department of Archives and History, 1430 Senate Street, Columbia, 29211.

South Dakota State Historical Society, Soldiers and Sailors Memorial Building, Pierre, 57501.

Tennessee Historical Commission, 403 Seventh Avenue, North Nashville, 37219.

Texas Library and Historical Commission, 1201 Brazos, Box 12927 Capitol Station, Austin, 78711.

Utah State Historical Society, 603 E. South Temple, Salt Lake City, 84102.

Vermont Historical Society, Pavilion Building, Montpelier, 05602.

Virginia Historical Society, 428 North Boulevard, Richmond, 23221.

Washington State Historical Society, 315 North Stadium Way, Tacoma, 98403.

West Virginia Department of Archives and History, 400 East Wing, State Capitol, Charleston, 25305.

State Historical Society of Wisconsin, 816 State Street, Madison, 53706.

Wyoming State Archives and History Department, State Office Building, Cheyenne, 82001.

### Research and Study Guides in History

If you wish to consult a history study guide written for more advanced students, here is a list of some publications.

Wood Gray, *Historian's Handbook: A Key to the Study and Writing of History.* Boston: Houghton Mifflin, 1964.

Norman Cantor and Richard Schneider, *How to Study History.* New York: T. Y. Crowell, 1967.

Robert Daniels, *Studying History: How and Why,* Englewood Cliffs, N.J.: Prentice-Hall, 1972.

Robert Shafer, *A Guide to Historical Method.* Homewood, Ill.: Dorsey, 1974.

### Grammar and Style Manuals

If you know that your background in grammar and composition is weak, or if you need more specific information concerning report writing, here are a few manuals that should help.

Jacques Barzun and Henry Graff, *The Modern Researcher.* New York: Harcourt Brace Jovanovich, 1970.
Cecil B. Williams, *A Research Manual for College Studies and Papers.* New York: Harper & Row, 1963.
University of Chicago Press, *A Manual of Style.* Chicago: University of Chicago Press, 1969.
Kate L. Turabian, *A Manual for Writers of Term Papers, Theses, and Dissertations.* Chicago: University of Chicago Press, 1973.

### Call Numbers: The Library of Congress System

The identification system of the Library of Congress divides the major subject classifications by letter. The following are the Library of Congress subject categories and their respective letter designations.

A  General works
B  Philosophy, psychology, religion
C  Auxiliary sciences of history
D  General and Old World history
E  American (Western Hemisphere) history
F  American history (continued)
G  Geography, anthropology, customs, sports
H  Social sciences, economics, socialism
J  Political science, international law
K  Law
L  Education
M  Music
N  Fine arts
P  Language, literature
Q  Science
R  Medicine
S  Agriculture
T  Technology
U  Military science
V  Naval science
Z  Bibliography, library science

Each letter group is broken down further by the addition of a second letter and then by numbers. Here are some of the breakdowns of the categories D, E, and F, which deal with history.

D            General history
DA           Great Britain
                 20–690 England
                 700–745 Wales
                 750–890 Scotland
                 900–995 Ireland
DB           Austria-Hungary
DC           France
DD           Germany
DE           Classical antiquity
DF           Greece
DG           Italy
DH-DJ        Netherlands
                 DH     1–207 Belgium and Holland
                 DH    401–811 Belgium
                 DH    901–925 Luxemburg (grand duchy)
                 DJ     Holland
DK           Russia
                 1–272 Russia (general)
                 401–441 Poland
                 445–465 Finland
                 750–891 Russia in Asia
DL           Scandinavia
                 1– 85 Scandinavia (general)
                 101–291 Denmark
                 301–398 Iceland
                 401–596 Norway
                 601–991 Sweden
DP           Spain and Portugal
                 1–402 Spain
                 501–900 Portugal
DQ           Switzerland
DR           Turkey and the Balkan States
DS           Asia
DT           Africa
DU           Australia and Oceania
DX           Gypsies

E   America (General) and United States (General)
         11–143 America (general)

31– 45 North America (general)
51– 99 Indians of North America
101–135 Discovery of America
151–810 United States
151–185 General history and description
185 Negroes in the United States
186–199 Colonial period
201–298 Revolution
351–364 War of 1812
401–415 War with Mexico
441–453 Slavery
458–655 Civil War
482–489 Confederate States
714–735 War with Spain

F    United States (local) and America except the United States
1– 970 United States (local)
1001–1140 British North America, Canada, Newfoundland
1201–1392 Mexico
1401–1419 Latin America (general)
1421–1577 Central America
1601–2151 West Indies
2201–2239 South America (general)
2251–2299 Colombia
2301–2349 Venezuela
2351–2471 Guiana: British, Dutch, French
2501–2659 Brazil
2661–2699 Paraguay
2701–2799 Uruguay
2801–3021 Argentine Republic
3051–3285 Chile
3301–3359 Bolivia
3401–3619 Peru
3701–3799 Ecuador

Thus a volume whose call number begins DK 408 deals with Polish history, and one which begins E 451 is about the history of slavery in the United States.

### Call Numbers: The Dewey Decimal System

The Dewey system is a decimal system. There are ten main subject headings, each containing 100 different numbers:

000–099 General works
100–199 Philosophy
200–299 Religion
300–399 Social sciences
400–499 Language
500–599 Pure science
600–699 Technology
700–799 The arts
800–899 Literature
900–999 History

Each of the main subject divisions is itself divided into ten sections of ten units each. The divisions of history are:

900–909 General history
910–919 Geography, travel, description
920–929 Biography
930–939 Ancient history
940–949 European history
950–959 Asian history
960–969 African history
970–979 North American history
980–989 South American history
990–999 Other regions of the world

Each of these divisions is further divided into ten parts. The divisions of 970 to 979 (North American history), for example, are as follows:

970 General North American history
971 Canadian history
972 Mexican and Caribbean history
973 General United States history
974 Northeastern states, U.S.
975 Southeastern states, U.S.
976 South-central states, U.S.
977 North-central states, U.S.
978 Western states, U.S.
979 Far-western states, U.S. and Alaska

Thus a volume whose call number begins with 934 deals with ancient history, and one that begins with 978 is concerned with the history of one or more of the western states of the United States.

### Common Abbreviations Used in Footnotes, Bibliographies, Catalogs, and Reference Books

| | |
|---|---|
| anon. | anonymous |
| app. | appendix |
| art. | article (plural, arts.) |
| b. | born |
| bk. | book (plural, bks.) |
| bull. | bulletin |
| c. | copyright |
| ca. | *circa*, about, approximately. Used with approximate dates, e.g., "ca. 1804." |
| cf. | *confer*, compare. Used only when the writer wishes the reader to compare two or more works. |
| ch. or chap. | chapter (plural, chaps.) |
| col. | column (plural, cols.) |
| comp. | compiler (plural, comps.) |
| d. | died |
| diss. | dissertation |
| ed. | edition, editor (plural, eds.) |
| e.g. | *exempli gratia*, for example |
| enl. | enlarged |
| et al. | *et alia*, and others |
| et seq. | *et sequens*, and the following |
| fac. | facsimile |
| fig. | figure (plural, figs.) |
| ibid. | *ibidem*, in the same place |
| id. | *idem*, the same (person) |
| i.e. | *id est*, that is |
| ill. | illustrated, illustration |
| infra | below (referring to a later point in the work) |
| l. or ll. | line(s) |

| | |
|---|---|
| loc. cit. | *loco citato,* in the place cited (referring to the same passage cited in an immediately previous footnote) |
| MS | manuscript (plural, MSS) |
| n. | note, footnote (plural, nn.) |
| n.d. | no date (of publication is given) |
| no. | number (plural, nos.) |
| n.p. | no place (of publication) or no publisher (is given) |
| n.s. | new series |
| o.p. | out of print |
| op. cit. | *opere citato,* in the work cited |
| o.s. | old series |
| p. | page (plural, pp.) |
| par. | paragraph (plural, pars.) |
| passim | here and there (throughout the work cited) |
| pseud. | pseudonym |
| pt. | part (plural, pts.) |
| q.v. | *quod vide,* which see |
| rev. | revised |
| sc. | scene |
| *sic* | so, thus (Enclosed in brackets to indicate an error or unusual statement in a quotation.) |
| supp. | supplement (plural, supps.) |
| supra | above (referring to an earlier point in the work) |
| trans. | translator |
| v. | verse (plural, vv.) |
| viz. | *videlicet,* namely |
| vol. | volume (plural, vols.) |
| vs. | *versus,* against |